IT'S ALL ABOUT CLOUT

ABOUT THE AUTHOR

Max Foster is a CNN anchor and reporter based in London with nearly thirty years' experience in broadcasting. He hosts the global debate show 'CNN Talk with Max Foster' which appears on CNN International, Facebook and iTunes. He also anchors the London edition of the newscast 'CNN Newsroom.'

Max has played a pivotal role in CNN's coverage of major world events, often on location, and has interviewed influential leaders and trail blazers from Donald Trump and Steve Jobs to Taylor Swift. He is also CNN's Royal Correspondent and London Correspondent. He led the network's reporting on the UK 'Brexit' referendum and his royal exclusives include interviews with The Duke of Cambridge, The Prince of Wales and The Queen of Denmark.

Max is a speaker and moderator for various international bodies, including the United Nations. He runs masterclasses in news anchoring for CNN affiliates around the world and he blogs at 'cloutology.com' on matters relating to this book.

WITH RARE INSIGHT
FROM SOME OF THE WORLD'S
MOST PROMINENT PEOPLE

IT'S ALL ABOUT
CLOUT

cloutology.com

CNN'S MAX FOSTER

DEDICATION

For Hannah, Albert, Nancy, Walter and my mother Ingrid. Thank you for your support and (near) unwavering patience for the job I love.

CONTENTS

ACKNOWLEDGEMENTS

Thank you to CNN for allowing me to write this book on their watch and for granting me the experiences that informed it. Thank you to the people I write about for letting me into their lives, even if it was only fleeting. Thank you to Melissa Marshall for introducing me to the world of book writing and Vanessa Fox O'Loughlin at The Inkwell Group who helped me knock it into shape with Afric McGlinchey.

INTRODUCTION

'Who is the most interesting person you have ever met?'

It's a question I am often asked in my role as a news anchor and reporter and I always give the same names: 'Steve Jobs,' 'Donald Trump,' 'The Queen' …

At some point, I started asking myself: Why them? Why not other high-profile people I have worked with?

Those that came to mind had influence and a certain degree of power but I couldn't narrow it down any further than that, until I had a eureka-in-the-shower moment and realised they all had 'clout.'

Clout is a difficult thing to define but you know when it's there. I think of it as the power to attract an audience and influence them but it's more emotional than that.

To test my theory, I tried an experiment on friends. I asked them to name people they knew who had clout. Their answers came instinctively, and they were as quick to dismiss people who *didn't* have clout as they were to name those that *did*. If they identified someone junior to them as having clout, then that person would suddenly go up in their estimations. If they named someone senior as lacking clout then it would have the opposite effect. Clout then wasn't necessarily related to seniority but it was a strong indicator of potential and leadership quality.

This wasn't a particularly scientific study, I accept, but it was enough to reassure me that I was on to something with this book. 'You're right,' one friend told me, 'it's all about clout.' And with that, I had my title.

My mission was then to explore *why* certain people had clout and my first question there was whether it was learned or came naturally. The more I studied the people I considered to have clout, the more I realised what different characters they were. Some were outgoing, some shy, others smart. They didn't fit in to any particular category or personality type so it must be something that was learned.

I was then able to establish what people with clout *did* have in common and whilst I can't give you an exact recipe for this elusive quality, I can offer a list of the key ingredients. As a mnemonic device, I have made sure they all start with the letter 'C':

CAUSE

CREDIBILITY

CHARACTER

CONVERSATION

CONNECTION

CACHET

I've dedicated a chapter of this book to each of these 6Cs and illustrate with individuals who have had an impact on me. In the final chapter, I will bring it together and explain how you can use the same model to develop your own clout.

I focus on famous people because I want to give you examples that you can relate to, but clout isn't necessarily to do with how well-known you are. The special advisors, talent agents and hedge fund managers of this world wield immense clout from behind the scenes, and you will know people in your community who have clout but aren't more widely known.

I don't have a personal relationship with any of the people I have written about and none have collaborated with this book. I simply took their public profiles – which is where their clout exists – and added any context from my own interactions and experiences with them.

This isn't a memoir. It's *my* interpretation of relevant experiences. The teams I worked with at the time will have their own view on what transpired and that's why I have left their names out. I will do their contributions justice if I do write that memoir. Suffice to say, I wouldn't be able to do this job without the people around me.

You could call this a self-help book but you might find it has a slightly unusual format. I deliberately avoided studying the market because I wanted to stay as true as I could to my own first-hand experience, rather than being swayed by what's already out there.

I've seen how people with clout aren't held back by convention and it's in that spirit that I also decided to self-publish. It's been a thoroughly lonely experience but, by leaving my comfort zone, I have gained a new perspective on life and what it takes to succeed. I hope you find this book useful.

CHAPTER 1

STEVE JOBS
CAUSE

'There's an old Wayne Gretzky quote that I love. "I skate to where the puck is going to be, not where it has been," and we've always tried to do that at Apple since the very, very beginning and we always will.'

Steve Jobs, MacWorld, 9 January 2007[1]

STEVE JOBS WAS BORN, 24 February 1955, to two University of Wisconsin students who gave him up for adoption. He was raised in California by his adoptive parents and dropped out of college to co-found Apple in 1979 from a garage with his friend Steve Wozniak.

Jobs was forced out of Apple in 1985 following a power struggle and went on to help launch Pixar Animations and the NeXT computer business. On his return to Apple in the late 1990s he reoriented the entire business around a new line-up of digital devices and the company went on to become the most valuable company in the world by market capitalisation.[2]

'Do you want to interview Steve Jobs?' I was asked by a planning producer as I stumbled deliriously out of the CNN London studio after my morning show on 2 April 2007.

I had been on air for three hours and my first port of call would usually have been the bathroom but I stopped, registered what the producer was saying and replied, 'Yes. Of course.'

Who *didn't* want to interview Steve Jobs?!

'We've just heard he's in London,' she added. 'And he's available for interview this morning. I'll organise a crew, and car to take you over.'

'Great, thanks,' I replied. 'I'll meet them in reception, after I've been to the loo.'

On the way over to West London to meet Jobs, I reflected on what I knew about him. He was more than a business leader; he was a cultural icon and I was about to interview him at a pivotal point in his career. He'd just unveiled his most fantastical gadget yet – the iPhone – and it was about to go on sale. None of us had seen anything like it before and we didn't know how the market would take it. It promised, amongst other things, a 'touch screen' which was positively space-aged for my button-pressing generation.

I was aware the iPhone was a huge investment for Apple and a personal gamble for Jobs who had staked his reputation on its success. He had been intimately involved in the design.

It didn't quite add up that he wanted to come all the way to London though, at such a critical time for the business. All I had been told was that he'd signed a deal with the music label, EMI which didn't feel big enough to justify the trip.

When I arrived, with my cameraman, at EMI head-quarters in Kensington, we bundled our equipment out of the taxi on to the pavement and wheeled it in to reception. Other crews were already waiting to speak to Jobs. It clearly wasn't an exclusive.

The lobby was cavernous. I looked up to the high ceiling and out through the atrium to the grey London sky. Hip staff were scurrying around, talking music and gigs.

EMI was a powerhouse in music, one of the 'big four' global recording companies with a pedigree going back to the Beatles. These were hallowed walls in the world of contemporary music.

A press officer came over and handed me a press release, which took some making-sense-of in my post-programme haze:

'**London – April 2nd, 2007**. Apple today announced that EMI Music's entire digital catalogue of music will be available for purchase DRM-free (without digital rights management) from the iTunes Store worldwide in May. DRM-free tracks from EMI will be offered at higher quality 256 kbps AAC encoding, resulting in audio quality indistinguishable from the original recording, for just 99 pence per song…'[3]

That was as far as I got before having to go back and re-read it. I was a business reporter by trade so I knew a bit about the dynamics of the music and tech sectors but this was like reading code.

The labels were making most of their money from physical sales of compact discs. The growth was in digital downloads but they couldn't turn enough of a profit because of rampant piracy.

The industry had come together to fight the pirates with a technology called Digital Rights Management (DRM) which was embedded in to music to prevent it being shared. DRM was a very expensive system to operate and, more worryingly, the pirates kept finding ways around any updates.

I was also aware that music fans didn't like DRM because it reduced sound quality and would only allow them to play their digital music collections on a limited range of devices. Steve Jobs had stepped in on their behalf with an open letter earlier that year calling for the end of DRM. 'Imagine a world where every online store sells DRM-free music encoded in open, licensable formats,' he wrote. 'In such a world, any player can play music purchased from any store, and any store can sell music which is playable on all players. This is clearly the best alternative for consumers, and Apple would embrace it in a heartbeat.'[4]

That's when Jobs' trip to London starts making sense. EMI was the first major label to act in response to the letter by dropping DRM. The other labels weren't at all happy with EMI at the time and Jobs must have come over to show support for EMI's pioneering spirit, and perhaps nudge a few of its competitors in to following suit.

Eventually, my cameraman and I were picked up from EMI reception and taken up to the boardroom. It was dominated by a vast oval-shaped table with contemporary artwork hanging on the walls. In the corner was a makeshift TV studio comprising of two stools and a sheet of black fabric draped behind. Steve Jobs was sitting on one stool, Eric Nicoli, the CEO of EMI, on the other.

Jobs was wearing his signature outfit: jeans, sneakers, and a long-sleeved black T-shirt. Nicoli was a more visible presence, in a formal pink shirt with grey trousers, as if he had removed his suit jacket and tie to get-down with Jobs' more casual look.

As my cameraman set up his shot, I offered a hand-shake to both and introduced myself. Jobs immediately leaned in to me and launched into a mesmerising pitch about why the EMI deal was a no-brainer for everyone concerned. I usually have to warm my guests up before an interview but Jobs was straight in there, eyes locked on mine. It wasn't intimidating – more of a charm offensive, and I have to say it worked. I was young and flattered to be at the centre of his attention – this was one of the world's most powerful people.

Once the camera was rolling, Jobs went back over what he had told me with even more gusto.

'Here's the thing,' he explained. 'Ninety per cent of music today is shipped on CDs without DRM. So, what we are announcing today is that we are putting the digital world on par with the CD.'

He was animated, a slight smile, utterly focused and he punctuated each thought with an animated, often dramatic arm gesture. If you turned the volume down on the interview he would have appeared eccentric, but from his voice you knew he was in full control.

Jobs spoke with purpose, adjusting the pace of what he was saying to make sure I was keeping up. He monitored my concentration levels with his eyes. I could tell, it was fine. I wanted to understand. It was an education for me, which I suspect is how he regarded it too.

When I brought Nicoli in to the interview, the energy levels sank. You might argue he was at a disadvantage: the reserved Brit pitted against the cool, charismatic Californian but Jobs was anything but relaxed, he was intense. When I brought the questions back to him, he fired the conversation up again, explaining how music downloads represented only 10 per cent of the market but that it was growing at 100 per cent a year.

'To accelerate that growth, so it can make up for the decline in the physical CD sales,' he said, 'we are closing the gap between the digital and CD worlds by removing the digital DRM and by increasing the audio quality.'

EMI desperately needed growth. Nicoli and his board were under intense pressure from shareholders to make up for dwindling sales of CDs. He needed to show they could do something bold in the digital space and iTunes was the 'shiny new thing' at the time, as one insider described it to me years later. Nicoli took a gamble and threw his lot in with Apple. By doing so, he was putting his faith in Jobs to deliver on his promises.

'It's been really successful so far,' Jobs continued in the interview. 'We want to keep it going and even accelerate its growth towards some day when the majority of music is sold digitally over the internet versus all this physical stuff that we have today.'

It was starting to sound more like a manifesto to save the music industry than a corporate announcement, and that's exactly what Jobs intended. He was making clear that this wasn't about him, or even Apple; it was about anyone and everyone who had a stake in a healthy, wealthy music sector.

The idea that digital sales would ever overtake CDs was difficult for any of us to imagine at the time, despite the industry trends. Most music buyers were still enjoying the ritual of going down to the record store and browsing through CDs, soaking up the cover art along the way. Jobs was suggesting we all give that up and stay at home to download our music on to a computer instead, and one track at a time. That threatened not only the tradition of the music store but the concept of the album itself. For music purists, this was blasphemy. The album was an art-form in their minds, carefully crafted to enhance the listening experience. Why would anyone want to pluck random tracks out and listen to them on a computer?

Jobs was never one for convention though and he also had a knack for knowing what customers wanted even before they even knew themselves.

Within seven years, by 2014, music downloads had indeed overtaken CD sales and record stores had become a rarity. Moreover, most music sales had shifted to iTunes and that made Jobs the most powerful figure in music. His industry takeover caught many music execs off guard but that was because it was a technological, not a musical, revolution and that was Jobs' turf.

Meeting Jobs remains one of the standout moments of my career, and not just because he was so well-known. I have met other famous and/or powerful people who haven't left the same impression with me.

I remember everything about Jobs, from what he said to how he said it and even what he wore. I had to dig-up a recording of the interview to gather any of that information on Eric Nicoli.

It was the poet Maya Angelou who said: 'At the end of the day, people won't remember what you said or did, they will remember how you made them feel.'

Steve Jobs made me feel important, as though I had a contribution to make to his mission. I am usually pretty good at resisting that sort of influence and it didn't affect the interview but it was the way he leaned towards me from his stool and locked eyes, the gestures, the smile. There was an openness and honesty to him that was undeniably compelling. The sneakers and jeans added to his authenticity, as did his passion for what he was selling. But the thing that really marked him out was that sense of mission. He was the most driven person I have ever met, and I wasn't the first person to feel that.

I have yet to meet anyone with clout who wasn't also a disrupter. Jobs refused to be held back by what other people thought was possible. Perhaps he always felt like a misfit, having been adopted, but we certainly know he rebelled as a teenager.

'My mother taught me to read early so I was pretty bored in school, and I turned into a little terror,' Jobs told David Sheff in an interview for *Playboy* magazine in 1985. 'You should have seen us in third grade. We basically destroyed our teacher. We would let snakes loose in the classroom and explode bombs.'[5]

Jobs conformed enough to go to college but dropped out to set up Apple from a garage with his friend Steve Wozniak. Going into business 'was the chance to actually try something, to fail, to succeed, to grow,' he told Sheff.[6]

Jobs was never one for convention, explaining to *PBS* in 2011 that, 'When you grow up you tend to get told the world is the way it is and your job is just to live your life inside that world. Try not to bash into the walls too much. Try to have a nice family, have fun, save a little money. That's a very limited life. Life can be much broader once you discover one simple fact: everything around you that you call life was made up by people who were no smarter than you and you can change it, you can influence it, you can build your own things that other people can use. Once you learn that, you'll never be the same again.'[7]

Jobs certainly knew how to build his own thing. Apple turned over $200,000 in its first year, $7m in its second then $17m, $47m, $117m, $335m and $583m respectively, until in 1983 they were just shy of $1bn.

But it wasn't about the money.

'Being the richest man in the cemetery doesn't matter to me,' Jobs told the *Wall Street Journal* in 1993. 'Going to bed at night saying we've done something wonderful... that's what matters to me.'[8]

Jeff Goodell at *Rolling Stone* followed up on that thought up with Jobs the following year:

> **Goodell:** You said that the goal is not to be the richest guy in the cemetery. What is the goal?
>
> **Jobs**: I don't know how to answer you. In the broadest context, the goal is to seek enlightenment – however you define it. But these are private things. I don't want to talk about this kind of stuff.
>
> **Goodell:** Why?
>
> **Jobs**: I think, especially when one is somewhat in the public eye, it's very important to keep a private life.[9]

But Jobs had revealed enough to show the scale of his ambition. Enlightenment is perhaps the ultimate goal because it's unachievable. How do you ever make complete sense of the world? If you combine that with Jobs' philosophy to live each day as if it were his last, you begin to understand where his drive came from.

In a commencement speech at Stanford University in 2005, Jobs describes how, from the age of 17, he had looked in the mirror every morning and asked himself: 'If today were the last day of my life, would I want to do what I am about to do today?' That awareness of his own mortality was his 'most important tool' in making big choices in life 'because almost everything – all external expectations, all pride, all fear of embarrassment or failure – these things just fall away in the face of death, leaving only what is truly important. Remembering that you are going to die is the best way I know to avoid the trap of thinking you have something to lose. You are already naked. There is no reason not to follow your heart.'

What he also did there was reveal what he feared – 'embarrassment or failure.' We don't learn where that came from but it was clearly something that played on his mind throughout his career. That fear of failure drove him towards his goal of 'enlightenment.'

In 1985, when Jobs spoke to *Playboy*, he was 29, already a millionaire but dissatisfied with the way he had lost control of Apple. John Sculley was CEO at the time and he had overseen a drop off in Macintosh computer sales. The company was also heading for its first ever loss which must have been excruciating for Jobs to witness.

He appears to use his *Playboy* interview to set out an alternative vision for the company which was to put it at the vanguard of what he called the 'information revolution.'

'It's very crude today, yet our Macintosh computer takes less power than a 100-watt light bulb to run and it can save you hours a day. What will it be able to do ten or twenty years from now, or fifty years from now? This revolution will dwarf the petrochemical revolution. We're on the forefront.'

Like all revolutionaries, Jobs needed an established order to rise up against and for him that was IBM – the dominant force in personal computing at the time. The killer app in the market was word processing and Jobs argued that his Mac was far superior to an IBM because you didn't need to understand code to use it. You could also express yourself creatively on a Mac by changing the font and adding pictures and graphs. The whole system was more intuitive. Macs even had a 'mouse' that you could use to point to where you wanted to go on the screen instead of having to tap furiously away at the arrow keys.

Apple didn't just compete on capability but on function and look. You could imagine a stylish Mac in your home more than a workmanlike IBM. A Mac was a status symbol and your stake in the information revolution.

Few of Jobs' ideas were entirely new and he never pretended otherwise. 'Picasso had a saying,' he told *PBS* in 1996. 'He said, "Good artists copy, great artists steal." And we have always been shameless about stealing great ideas.'[10]

He took existing innovations, made them better and then protected the designs ferociously so nobody could copy them. It made Apple a very exciting company to work for.

'We attract a different type of person,' Jobs told Sheff, 'someone who really wants to get in a little over his head and make a little dent in the universe. We are aware that we are doing something significant.'[11]

He could be difficult to work for and he didn't always get it right. His notable flops included the Apple III and Lisa computers. Jobs didn't let his fear of failure beat him though. He used it as a source of strength, vowing to learn from his mistakes.

'Much of what I stumbled into by following my curiosity and intuition turned out to be priceless later on,' Jobs told the students at the Stanford.[12]

It was a lesson he most famously learned shortly after his *Playboy* interview when he launched his bid to unseat John Sculley as CEO. The plan leaked and Sculley convened the board, calling a vote of confidence, which Jobs lost and he ran out of the room in tears.[13]

'It was awful-tasting medicine,' Jobs said later, 'but I guess the patient needed it. Sometimes life hits you in the head with a brick. Don't lose faith. I'm convinced that the only thing that kept me going was that I loved what I did.'[14]

He dusted himself down and reinvented himself as a Hollywood studio boss with the hugely successful Pixar Animations. He also set-up another computer business, NeXT, which developed such a good operating system that Apple wanted to buy it. Jobs seized the opportunity to return to the company he co-founded and went with the NeXT. Once he was back at Apple he wasted little time launching his second boardroom coup and this time he won, successfully unseating Gil Amelio as CEO in 1997.

Jobs reoriented the business around a new line of digital products fit for the information revolution including the iPod and iTunes. 'One of the biggest insights we had was that we decided not to try to manage your music library on the iPod, but to manage it in iTunes,' he told *Newsweek* in 2006. 'Other companies tried to do everything on the device itself and made it so complicated that it was useless.'[15]

iTunes became central to Apple strategy but it took years to get right. When I interviewed him at EMI in 2007 it still wasn't working in the way he intended. He was about to launch the iPhone and one of its selling points was that users could access their music on the go at high quality and on a device of their choice. DRM was getting in the way of that which is why he was so fired up when I met him. DRM was an obstacle to the iPhone's success so it was a huge moment for him when EMI agreed to drop it and sell unrestricted through iTunes.

When the iPhone went on sale, it flew off the shelves. I was one of those reporting on the long queues outside Apple stores around the world. Customers camped out for days to get to the front. It felt more like a pilgrimage.

In 2016, Apple sold its billionth iPhone,[16] making it one of the best-selling products of all time. Steve Jobs was perhaps the only person who could have imagined that happening but he didn't live to see it.

Following a long battle with pancreatic cancer, Steve Jobs died on 5th October 2011, at the age of 56.

One of Apple's original employees, Bud Tribble, described what he called a 'reality distortion field' around Jobs: 'In his presence, reality is malleable. He can convince anyone of practically anything.'[17]

If you're seeking enlightenment and you refuse to be held back by convention then there's very little stopping you. Combine that with Jobs' fear of failure and you can see how he was so driven to succeed.

He threw all that energy in to a cause that he could champion and customers, staff, shareholders, the board and even the media could get behind too – the 'information revolution.'

He always spoke in terms of 'we' and 'us,' not 'me' and 'I' to make it a shared mission. Everyone had a stake in it. When he made a prediction about technology that came true then his entire audience felt vindicated and proud.

Jobs was an almost spiritual figure. We all looked to him for guidance on where technology was going next, which was an extraordinary achievement. He was the one CEO who could hold a product launch and the world media would turn up without even knowing what it was about. He owned the technology conversation and it was his sense of cause that underpinned his clout.

Jobs' Cloutfile

Cause: The 'information revolution'.

Credibility: He co-founded the world's most valuable company from a garage and proved himself when predictions came true.

Character: Authentic and true to his cause.

Conversation: He spoke convincingly to where technology was going next and how it would look.

Connection: He made his brand aspirational for both customers and staff.

Cachet: He was the world's most influential futurologist.

CHAPTER 2

TRACEY EMIN
CREDIBILITY

'I worked for this. I made this happen and I want to show other people they can do that.'
Tracey Emin, Desert Island Discs,
BBC Radio 4, 3 February 2004.[18]

TRACEY EMIN WAS BORN IN London in 1963 and was brought up in the English seaside town of Margate. Her Turkish-Cypriot father split his time between two families but walked out on Emin, her twin brother and mother when the family hotel business collapsed.

Despite leaving school at 13, Emin won a place at the world-renowned Royal College of Art in London. She made her name first as one of the Young British Artists that were showcased in the landmark *Sensation* exhibition at The Royal Academy of Arts in 1997. She was appointed Professor of Drawing at the Academy in 2011 and awarded a CBE by The Queen in 2013.

It was the autumn of 1997 and I had moved from Bath to London for a reporting position at the BBC World Service. I was making the most of all the capital had to offer and the talk of the town was a new exhibition at the Royal Academy of Arts called *Sensation*. It had been drawn from the contemporary art collection of advertising guru Charles Saatchi. One piece in particular had caused an uproar and Fellows of the Academy had even threatened to walk out over it.

'Myra,' by Marcus Harvey, portrayed an infamous police mugshot of the child killer, Myra Hindley. The most horrifying thing about it was the way it was made up of rubber handprints cast from children. On the opening day of the exhibition, there were protests outside, supported by a mother of one of Hindley's victims. Windows were smashed and vandals managed to get inside to throw paint and eggs at the canvas, prompting security to be increased. It was the journalist in me as much as the art fan that wanted to go and see the show for myself.

The 1990s were defined in many ways by what I would describe as a rush to authenticity. It affected every type of media. The more shocking and raw the content, the more the public wanted it. It was the same zeitgeist that gave rise to reality TV and the paparazzi.

When I arrived at the Academy for the show, I had to strain to see the artwork due to the size of the crowds attending. The one exhibit that was impossible to miss was 'Myra' because it was huge. Her eyes peered menacingly at me over people's heads. As I moved towards her, the handprints came into view and my heart went out to the mother who had been protesting outside. How could an artist have conceived this? What possessed the gallery to hang it? Why had I paid to view it?

I stood, staring for while then just moved on, not wanting to make any more sense of it. I don't think art should be censored but I sympathised with why people wanted it taken down. Hindley was already a hate figure and this only made her crimes feel rawer.

As I moved through the rest of the exhibition, there was more shock to behold. A photo of an old man sitting in a chair in squalid conditions, ducking out of the way of a cat being flung over his head. It was taken by Richard Billingham in his family home. The old man was his father who was a long-term alcoholic.

Then there was the self-portrait by Marc Quinn – a bust, shaped out of 10 pints of his own, frozen blood. The 'mutilated mannequins' by the Chapman brothers were so offensive, that they had to be exhibited in an adult-only section. By the time I reached Damien Hirst's famous pickled shark I was so desensitised I just lingered there, my mind drifting away into the blue formaldehyde…

The piece that had the most lasting impact on me though didn't scream at you like the others. It was a small blue tent pitched in the middle of one of the gallery spaces, called 'Everyone I Ever Slept With 1963 – 1995,' by Tracey Emin.

I remember kneeling down to have a look inside and seeing lots of names sewn in to the inner walls: 'Billy Childish,' 'Frank Berbee,' 'Tracey Horn'…

I assumed they were people she'd had sex with. It was so brutally honest it prompted me to question my own history and whether I could ever be so candid. It was as if the tent was talking to me, or was it Emin?

Later, I realised I had over-simplified the tent. The clue was in the mention of dates in the title: 'Everyone I Ever Slept With 1963 – 1995.'

1963 was the year Emin was born and one of names belonged to her twin brother, who she'd shared a womb with. Another was her grandmother who couldn't walk so Emin would climb into bed next to her when she went to visit. The tent was about intimacy within all kinds of relationships, not just sexual ones and that made it even more poignant.

Sensation made stars out of all the artists who exhibited there. Collectively, they became known as the 'YBAs' or Young British Artists. By the end of that year, Emin was breaking out on her own however, helped by a drunken appearance on late night TV.

She had been invited, along with various luminaries from the art world, to discuss that year's Turner art prize which had been awarded again to a video artist. 'Is painting dead?' was the rather high-minded topic of discussion and Emin just wasn't in the mood.

'I am the only artist here from that show Sensation,' Emin slurred, smoking furiously. 'I want to be with my friends. I'm drunk. I want to phone my mum. She's going to be embarrassed by this conversation. I don't care. I don't give a f*** about it.'[19]

There were sniggers, the panel tried to ignore her and she walked out. Emin had the last laugh though when the newspapers picked up on her appearance. *The Guardian* interpreted it as a piece of art in itself, 'The work was astutely timed. Video art has won the Turner two years in succession. This one will hardly need editing before getting what it richly deserves: next year's prize.'[20]

It was 13 years later when I had the chance to meet Emin myself, by which point I had left the BBC and was with CNN. It was the year she was appointed as a Fellow of the Royal Academy of Arts itself, the ultimate honour from the British art establishment. It had been an extraordinary journey.

With success came a grand new art studio Emin had built out of the shell of a disused factory in East London. I was the first reporter allowed in to film and I saw polished concrete floors, white-washed walls and towering windows bringing a wash of sunshine in from outside. In the basement there was even a swimming pool that she could use to paddle up and down to break through creative blocks.

She was working when we arrived so I suggested she carry on while we took some shots of the studio and set the camera up for the interview.

The space was immaculate. It would have felt clinical if it weren't for all the clutter. There were wooden pallets, an old bike and a ladder against the wall. In the middle of the room, a large wooden table stood proudly with tubes of paint lined up on it, in precise colour order. Three white storage boxes were stacked nearby but with the largest one on top, which felt counterintuitive. I found myself questioning what was art and what was waiting to be art. It was as if I was seeing everything through Emin's eyes suddenly. Was the red fabric sofa for sitting on or her next million-dollar masterpiece?

When the cameraman was ready, our producer brought Emin over and she said, 'You just start talking to me and I will just answer, that's the best thing,' she directed. An interviewee after my own heart.

She wore jeans and a smart black blouse with a delicate gold necklace. Her hair, shoulder length was flicked to the side away from me.

Emin had agreed to the interview because she was promoting a new series of watercolours she had produced in collaboration with the French-American artist Louise Bourgeois. I had asked that she bring out a couple of her favourite pieces so we could talk through them together and she had selected two brightly coloured male erections. One had an image of a woman dangling off the end of it, hanging limp from a rope around her neck.

'I thought this looked pretty tragic,' Emin told me. 'But I couldn't help but laugh when I did it. It was just, "How many women have felt like that, hey?"'

We giggled together, which is a very British coping mechanism. The image was graphic, to say the least.

'Felt like what?' I asked.

'Just hanging off the end of a man's penis, you know. It's like the end really.'

I didn't really know, but then I wasn't a woman. Emin's work is uncompromisingly honest at the best of times and even she admits it can be hard to live with, equating each piece to a mirror on her life.

'You couldn't live looking at a mirror the whole time. So, for me, with my work, I like to look at it for a while and then I like to pack it up and put it away because it makes me too fizzy, it makes me too churned up emotionally.'

To understand where she is coming from, you need to get past the initial shock and see each of her works as an act of therapy. She takes an emotion about intimacy and expresses it using whatever material and imagery she feels are most appropriate. It may take a lot of crafting or none. What matters is that each piece articulates her sentiments as accurately and honestly as possible. The creative process in itself allows Emin to come to terms with her own demons.

What makes her work resonate is that it taps in to universal emotions that we can all relate to. It prompts us to challenge our own feelings, just as the tent made me question my past. It's therapy for everyone, not just her and that's how she connects.

In her film 'Why I Never Became a Dancer,'[21] Emin reminisces about her upbringing in the English coastal town of Margate. Her medium is grainy archive footage and in the narration she describes how she left school at the age of 13 and whiled away her time away on the promenade.

'You'd go to the pub, you'd walk home, have fish and chips, then sex,' she says candidly. Home was with a brother, and single mother who worked all hours to make ends meet. Sex was with men up to twice her age whom she describes as 'pathetic.' It was an 'adventure, a 'learning,' she claims though we know at least one of those encounters can be classed as rape.

'By the time I was 15, I'd had them all and for me Margate was too small.' She throws her energy in to dancing instead, entering a local competition with high hopes of winning. If she got through, she might even make it big in London. Emin goes on stage and it starts well. She could hear people clapping. Then a group of men, all of whom she'd had sex with, start chanting insults. She runs out in tears, vowing to get out of Margate once and for all.

At the end of the film, Emin names and shames the chanting men and signs off with, 'This one's for you...' and we see her dancing as an adult with a big smile on her face.

While we might not all be able to identify with Emin's exact experience in Margate, we've all suffered teenage angst and that's how her audience identifies with her. Importantly, she shows how she survives and comes out stronger than before. The men didn't stop her dancing. She's living evidence of how you can come to terms with your past and move on. The film's about hope more than tragedy.

If dance wasn't Emin's ticket out of Margate then art would prove to be. She had taken a course in fashion but dropped out in favour of printmaking and then moved on to painting where she found herself.[22] The tutors were so impressed with her work, they encouraged her to apply to college. She didn't have the right qualifications because she had dropped out of school at such a young age but they let her in anyway. She excelled and graduated to the prestigious Royal College of Art, in London.

This was 1980s Britain. Margaret Thatcher was in power and the economy was booming. It's an era remembered in the UK for 'Yuppie' financial workers splashing their cash on fast cars, champagne and fine art. If students at the Royal College got their marketing right, they could put themselves on the fast track to fame and fortune. Art dealers would be invited in to preview student work and were known to buy up entire portfolios before they were even exhibited.

Emin was having none of it. 'I learned, if this is art, I don't want to know about it,' she told *The South Bank Show* in 2005.[23] 'If this is being an artist, it doesn't interest me.'

In a piece for the Royal College website, Emin describes how unhappy she was there: 'I always referred to it as 'debutantes' day out'. It was incredibly posh, and I felt at the time like a misfit and found it hard to make friends.'[24]

Despite being a student of painting at a world-renowned school, Emin rejected the medium altogether and tossed her entire body of work in to a skip.[25] Compounded by the trauma of an abortion, she started to question her very creativity.

'I couldn't go on doing art unless it meant something to me emotionally,' she told Will Self at *The Independent* in 1999, 'so I began making things out of bits of me.'[26]

Instead of creating stand-alone works of art to fit a mantelpiece or a plinth, Emin turned herself in to the canvas. Everything she produced became an expression of her – that mirror on her life. It was a completely new way of thinking about art and a blatant challenge to the established way of thinking.

Virtually penniless, she wrote letters asking people to invest £10 in her 'creative potential.' At a party she met an art dealer who had just set up his new gallery and he agreed to buy three of the letters. 'It totally shocked me,' says Jay Joplin. 'Great art does kind of punch you in the gut and spin your head and change the way you look at things. Getting those letters from Tracey was one of those moments.'[27]

Joplin agreed to represent her and he championed Emin's subversive influence from within the art firmament. If Steve Jobs was disrupting the world of technology, Emin was doing the same for British art.

The next time I met Emin was July 2014 at the Christie's auction house in London's upmarket Mayfair. Her most famous piece 'My Bed' was up for sale and it had been given pride of place in the centre of the preview show. There it was, under a spotlight in all its grotesque glory, surrounded by fascinated, sometimes bemused, onlookers.

It was conceived the year after *Sensation*, when Emin's relationship broke down. She had entered a deep depression and retreated to her bedroom in a social housing block.

'My Bed' is Emin's actual bed from the time, unpacked and recreated just as it was when she left it. Like many of her pieces, its power lies in its direct connection to a pivotal moment in her life. It's strewn with dirty sheets, used condoms and soiled underwear. On the floor around it are vodka bottles competing for space with pill packets, a pair of old slippers and an overflowing ashtray.

How often do you get to see anyone's unmade bed, let alone one as repulsive as this?

Then comes the self-questioning. Could I ever sink that low? How would I cope if I did? We've all been through nasty break-ups…

My thoughts were interrupted by Emin, wearing another black blouse, this time with a black jacket in keeping with the high-end setting. I explained that that we had met before but she didn't appear to remember which was slightly gutting.

She's relaxed in person, not the emotional wreck you see in her work. Perhaps she leaves it all in the studio, like the boxer who gets it out in the ring.

Emin: I actually spent 4 days in bed, not well and, feeling terrible and actually quite broken-hearted. I didn't eat and didn't drink anything and then when I finally got up to go and get a glass of water and staggered out to the kitchen, I came back and looked at this and thought, oh my God, that's kinda disgusting, I could have died in there.

And I looked again and I thought, it's not

disgusting; I didn't die. That bed kept me alive. And I had this sort of like vision of taking it out of the bedroom space and putting it in the gallery space and it just suddenly made sense, I thought, wow, this is a fantastic artwork.

Me: Do you mind if I ask why you were feeling the way you were at the time?

Emin: I was broken-hearted. Everyone's felt broken-hearted; it's not new. It's an accurate assessment of how I was at the time. So, I could do a drawing of myself but instead of that, I have this, and 16 years later it's still here, more iconic than ever.

Me: Are there bits of this that you unpacked and gave you a bit of a shudder?

Emin: I said it's a ghost of the self. When I sit on that bed I actually have, like a shudder of the past, going past me. It really is like a piece of history, like a time capsule. And I think people identify with it because most people have their own time capsules, if not in reality then in their memory or in their minds. So, I would like to be standing next to this in fifty years' time. That's what I hope.

Me: Well it's pretty much assured its place in art history, this piece, partly, I would say, because it epitomises that question of "What is art?" Because when you first produced this, they were saying it's not art.

Emin: OK.

Me: They're still saying it.

Emin: No, they're not.

Me: Is it art?

Emin: Course its art.

Me: It's your art.

Emin: It's not that. Any quiz show will ask the question: 'Which artist made the bed?' Tracey Emin

...

Taxi drivers: 'Oh, you're the artist that made the bed.'

They don't say to me, 'That isn't art,' they say you are the artist that made the bed.

Twenty years ago, this wasn't art; now it definitely is. It's changed people's perceptions of art and that's why it's a seminal piece of art, why it's important.[28]

Was she right? Well 'My Bed' sold for double the auction estimate, at a whopping £2,546,500 so the bidders were clearly convinced. If you could put a value on Emin's clout, this is it because there isn't any value in the bed.

When people say they could have done what she did and put their own bed in a gallery and put a million-dollar price tag on it, the point is they didn't and it wouldn't have made sense if they did. Emin's genius was in identifying how context gave the work resonance. 'My Bed' marked a turning point in her story, a fairy tale about a girl from a broken home who made it as an artist.

When a collector paid all that money for it, they weren't buying a dilapidated piece of old furniture, they were investing in an historical artefact. She had to put herself out there in the media so people could make sense of her story and how her pieces slot in to that. She is the opposite of the reclusive artist allowing the canvas to speak for itself. If she's the canvas, so she has to do the talking. Without her, the bed means nothing and she would have to pay someone to take it away.

'Art is an intensely personal journey,' she explained to me in her studio. 'It isn't there just to shake and provoke. It's there for to improve the soul.'

Emin wasn't the first artist to make us question what qualifies as art and she won't be the last but she did lead the conversation for a while which is where she earned her the cachet to command such high prices. She is, in her own words, a 'seminal' artist and she has a legitimate story to back that up. Her clout is rooted in her credibility as an artist.

'Whether people think it's good or bad or rubbish, I *have* done it,' she told Sue Lawley on the BBC's *Desert Island Discs* in 2004. 'That's what the difference is. Picasso did it with cubism.'[29]

Emin's Cloutfile

Cause: Redefining art.

Credibility: Self-made artist responsible for seminal works including the tent and bed. Fellow of the Royal Academy.

Character: Reliably, shockingly honest.

Conversation: What is intimacy? What is art?

Connection: Art as therapy for herself and her audience.

Cachet: Cover girl for the British art movement.

CHAPTER 3

STORMZY
CHARACTER

*'With where I come from, you're not really al-
lowed to talk in a certain way unless you've lived it
and unless that's actually you. Nothing can't really
be fabricated, people get found out quite quickly
in London. London's a bit of a jungle like that...
The listeners always want to hear, like, authentic
stuff, it doesn't have no street stuff or no gangster
stuff, they just wanna know that it's real.'*
Stormzy, Channel 4 News, 1 August 2015.[30]

Stormzy is a British-Ghanaian Grime artist from South
London. Born Michael Omari on 26th July 1993, he
was raised by a single mother with three siblings. He
started rapping, or MC'ing, at the age of 11 before,
was expelled from school and took a job as an engineer.
At the age of 19 he committed to a full-time music
career and was honoured at the prestigious *Mobo
Awards* in 2014, 2015 and 2017. In 2018, he won Best

Male Artist and Best Album for 'Gang Signs & Prayers' at the *Brits*.

––––––––––––

It was 22 February 2017 and I was on the red carpet which is one of my least favourite reporting positions but there were people there I was very keen to meet.

The Brit awards are the UK equivalent of the Grammy's and they are usually populated by mainstream acts backed by major labels. A new crop of home-grown talent had broken through though and without industry backing. Grime was their genre and it was born out of the streets of London in the early 2000s. It's defined by an MC rapping over instrumentals running at precisely 140 beats per minute. It's raw, aggressive and the two frontmen of the scene were there that night at the Brits.

Skepta decided to bypass the red carpet but Stormzy braved it. He wasn't easy to miss at 6 feet 5 inches tall, towering over the more recognisable pop and rock groups around him.

As he made his way along the line-up of reporters towards me, I listened in to what he was saying and it was a relief to hear him giving thoughtful, considered answers. Celebrities are all too often either too nervous or too dismissive to deliver on the red carpet. He was clearly more than capable of responding to my line of questioning.

When he came over to me, he was chewing gum and impeccably dressed in dark suit, white shirt and black tie. I didn't have long with him so I decided to skip the banter and cut straight to what I wanted to get explore with him.

Me: You've compared Grime to Rock'n'roll. Why do you think its hit the zeitgeist? What does it say about now?

Stormzy: The kids of our country are tuned in to what sounds real. You see, when the youth – kids and teenagers – are immersed in something, that's the truth.

Me: What does it say about culture?

Stormzy: It says we're just playing our part. We're here too. London, Grime music, the UK... we're just playing our part and we've been doing this for so long but it's just, like, the world's finally kinda said, oh hang on, what's happening there?

Me: America's catching on as well right, so what is it that resonates with them do you think?

Stormzy: I think it's just an authentic genre. It's an authentic genre of music. It's straight... it's un-edited, it's raw, it's not been filtered. Do you know what I mean? There's something about that, that's just universal, like whether you can understand the accent or you can get the tempo, that's universal, the rawness of it.[31]

And with that, Stormzy put his finger on why I think any media resonates. As with Emin's art, it has to feel honest. Audiences don't have care for content anymore they can't trust. There's so much choice they will just move on from you to someone who feels more honest.

'I don't want to have to put a mask on,' Stormzy told Sam Wolfson at *The Guardian* in 2016. "F*** that – sometimes I'm p****d off, sometimes f***** off, sometimes I'm up for banter, sometimes I can playfight for 12 straight hours with the mandem (friends).'[32]

It's that rawness that gives Stormzy his edge but it's also what makes him appealing. His core fanbase relates to him because he walks like them and talks like them. It's a wonder his music resonates anywhere outside the neighbourhood he originates from but it does because it has an air of authenticity that anyone can identify with. I've heard kids in rural middle-class areas reciting his words to the horror of their parents.

In his break-out *YouTube* hit, 'Shut Up,' Stormzy appears in his local park wearing a red tracksuit with a group of friends. You hear the early-2000s instrumental kick in and he looks slightly bashful before he finds his groove and begins freestyling, or adlibbing. His opening line is the killer and the one I hear recited most often, 'Man try say he's better than me, tell my man shut up!'[33] Then the pace picks up and Stormzy throws himself in. His energy sweeps up the entire group. They're bobbing to the beat and instinctively picking up the backing vocals. By the end of the track they are so united, the only way out of the music and back in to real life is for them to fall about laughing. It's spontaneous, it's endearing and it's palpably real. You don't have to know that park to connect with it.

The British boxer Anthony Joshua liked 'Shut Up' so much, he asked Stormzy to perform it ahead of one of his bouts at the *O2 Arena* in London. Then *BBC Radio 1* picked up on the track and the rest is Grime history.

At the time of writing, 'Shut Up' has been viewed more than 76 million times on *YouTube*.

The root of Stormzy's clout is in his strength of character and as it is for all of us, that's a product of his upbringing. He constantly refers to 'the ends' in his lyrics by which he means the neighbourhood in South London he grew up in.

'I hate being back in the ends,' he told Eleanor Halls at *GQ* magazine in 2016. 'My school was nasty, the kind of school where people go on to become convicted murderers.'

'I was a little prick,' he adds. 'I'd be the one to throw a sandwich at someone's head in assembly.'[34]

Stormy is smart. He achieved six A's at GCSE.[35] What his teachers didn't know was that he spent his school holidays in the public library. 'You read a book, write a detailed review as proof you've read it and they give you a badge,' he told *The Guardian*. 'That's where my competitive nature came out. Give me the badges! I would sit in the library all day, not 'cos I loved reading, just because I needed those badges.'[36]

He entered rap competitions at his local youth club from the age of 11.[37] 'My generation, me and my friends, we grew up on Grime,' he told Mark Savage at the BBC. 'We grew up in the era of Sony Ericsson phones, Walkman phones. There'd be a few Grime tunes circulating in the area and we'd send them to each other by Bluetooth. We used to listen to Krept and Konan, So Solid… These were all south London artists. People who were actually around me.'

At 13 he committed to stage name. 'I just thought, 'What's cool?'' A storm.'[38]

Music was an escape. 'Back then, I'm waking up, I'm hitting the roads, I'm going to get drugs, and I'm going to sell drugs, and I'm linking up with the mandem later, and we're going to figure out how to make some money tonight, where we can rob and who we can move to. And then you go home and you sleep,' he recalls to Miranda Sawyer at *The Observer*.

School didn't work out for him. He was expelled, then tried college and dropped out of that. He decided to leave London altogether in his late teens to pursue an apprenticeship in engineering in the English midlands and a good job came out of it – in quality assurance at an oil refinery. That wasn't for him either though. 'I didn't actually hand in my notice, I just left. I couldn't really tell my mum. I knew how she would take it!'[39]

Determined to avoid another failure, Stormzy returned to London and threw himself into his music. His legendary work ethic kicked in (the one from the library) and he left behind his life of crime, though it continued to inform his lyrics.

In the track 'Not That Deep,' Stormzy describes how he beat someone up in a sports store because they owed him money. In 'Mr Skeng,' he buys a gun aged 14. In 'Fight Things First,' he opens-up about his battle with depression.

His language may come across as tough and uncompromising but he's not afraid of showing his frailty either, which is where he connects with his audience, particularly men like him who lack role models willing to be so honest.

In 'Shut Up,' he aspires to make his mother proud and have enough money to send her on holiday. He pays tribute to her again to her in 'Lay Me Bare' but is uncompromisingly bitter about the father who walked out on them when Stormzy was a boy.

'Michael (Stormzy) is very intelligent,' his mother, Abigail Owuo, says in the book *This Is Grime*. 'He is a boy who has always said, "This is what I want," and he gets it. Not in a bad way. He was always the leader of his friends. If you follow him, you will fly. And the friends always followed him. By the time they are catching up, he is somewhere else, he is gone.'

Stormzy has remained close to those friends including Tobe Onwuka who is still his manager. The pair were approached by major music labels wishing to sign them but they resisted.

'From the outside looking in,' Onwuka told *GQ*'s Tom Lamont, 'labels are these places you go to as a musician and they make you. They do something. In these meetings I said, "So now we're here in front of you, what is this thing that you do?" And I never heard an answer. I never got it.'[40]

Stormzy and Onwuka created their own label instead, '#Merky,' though they draft in support from the majors as required for distribution. This has allowed Stormzy to develop independently as an artist and to avoid being sanitised to fit a certain segment of the market.

'Every single thing that I was told that I couldn't do without a label – get in the charts, get on to the Radio 1 playlist – I've done,' Stormzy told *The Guardian*.[41] 'The most important thing is to remain a good person, a good human,' he adds in *This Is Grime*. 'Forget fame or popularity, just being a good, decent human and a polite human is way more important than being the guy. Me being a good brother or a good son or a good friend or a good human means more than being a top MC.'[42]

In his music he can sound obsessed with money but being rich isn't his endgame. It's about escaping 'the ends' and taking his friends with him. That's the cause.

'How can I enjoy the luxuries and the glitz and the glamour when I've still got something to do? Because in my head, I can't sit down and say, "Mandem, we've done it. It's done." Not until all of my friends are millionaires. So nothing's done,' he tells *GQ*.[43]

'The ends' isn't as much a place as the sentiments it evokes. It's the hopelessness of being stuck in a rut where the only option is a life of crime that either lands you in prison or in the graveyard. It's the fear of returning to that that drives Stormzy and you can hear it in his lyrics.

'The main thing with me is my young black kings,' he tells *The Observer*. 'I need to talk to my young black kings, because I'm one of you, we who are always last. And I say to them, 'You are sick, you're nang, you can do this. You're better than anything anyone's ever told you that you are. You're just as powerful as me. You're just as sick as me. You are just as ambitious, and you can be just as creative and as incredible and as amazing as me, Kanye West, Drake, Frank Ocean, all these people that you see. You can do that.'[44]

When I met Stormzy at the Brits in 2017, I also had a chance to speak to Wiley, the so-called 'Godfather of Grime.' He's widely regarded as the creator of the genre and famously has labelled Stormzy 'the #1 grime don.'[45]

'The message is, it's about progression,' Wiley told me. 'You start somewhere in a place that's nowhere, you're trying to get somewhere. It's hard to get somewhere so you have to keep going and it takes a long time sometimes, though for some people it might happen quicker. If you have the star quality and you are ready to go now, it will happen now. God might give you another path where you have to do seven years before anyone notices, you know; everyone has different paths.'[46]

Stormzy embodied that notion and he came along at the right time to ride a resurgence in Grime of 2016. 'Grime is, in fact, the greatest music our city has ever, ever produced,' claims *Time Out London*. 'Sod punk. Sod jungle. Sod the Kinks and their soppy odes to bridge-based astronomy. There's one key thing that makes Grime more important than any other music from London, and that's that it's about much, much more than just music. It's about community.'[47]

Stormzy came from that community and spoke for it in a powerful way at the Brit Awards in 2018. He was the star of the show that year, winning two of the night's biggest honours and he used the platform to rap about an issue that plagues millions of Londoners – the housing crisis. He blasted the Prime Minister for failing those who had been left homeless after the 2017 Grenfell Tower housing block fire, which left 71 people dead. He branded Theresa May a criminal for ignoring their plight. 'Where's the money for Grenfell?' he called out from the stage.

His critique gained so much traction that the Prime Minister's office was forced to issue a statement the following day insisting that May was 'absolutely committed' to supporting people affected by Grenfell and that £58 million had been provided by the government.

Stormzy had gone mainstream and his message resonated to the lofty heights of the high-brow classical music network, Classic FM. A commentary on its website read: 'Stormzy joins a long list of composers throughout history who have sought to highlight the societal injustices around them, whether it's Russia under Stalin or segregated America. The point is, it's authentic: Stormzy's subject, the pursuit of justice for the survivors of the Grenfell Tower fire in West London, is one close to his heart, and that indignation comes across in his performance.'[48]

Less than two weeks after Stormzy called out the Prime Minister, she delivered a major speech on housing where she said young people were 'right to be angry' and she announced a series of reforms. The 'crisis of unafforda-bility,' May said, 'reinforces inequality. It prevents social mobility and stops people fulfilling their potential. It creates and exacerbates divisions between generations and between those who own property and those who do not.'[49] Stormzy couldn't have put it better himself.

When he was asked in 2015 where his career would be in 2018 he replied, 'I'll be the most prominent figure from our scene. And in terms of everything: success, music – everything! I think you're selling yourself short if you try and be anything less than that.'[50]

His Brits performance may have come from the gut but he's always had it in him. He's driven by a determination never to return to 'the ends' and to help other like him escape. He has the credibility to lead that conversation because he has been there, done that, but he's also proven his strength of character in his will to succeed. Everything he does speaks his cause and it feels genuine.

'My core is grime,' he told Eleanor Halls at *GQ*. 'But I make all kinds of music. Take Picasso. He could paint whatever way he liked. He could do a little ting with a felt tip if he wanted to – it's still going to be a bad boy Picasso at the end.'[51]

Stormzy's Cloutfile

Cause: Escaping 'the ends'.

Credibility: Self-made survivor, born out of the grass-roots of Grime.

Character: Raw, honest performances with a consistent message.

Conversation: Disenfranchisement and escape.

Connection: A role model for those wishing to follow in his path.

Cachet: The voice of Grime and the community it represents.

CHAPTER 4

EVA MOZES KOR
CONVERSATION

'Forgiveness is nothing more, nothing less than an act of self-healing, an act of reclaiming your life.'
Eva Kor, CNN, 1 February 2005

EVA MOZES KOR WAS BORN to a Hungarian-Jewish family in 1934. Her village was occupied by the Nazis when she was six and four years later they were all sent to the concentration camp at Auschwitz-Birkenau.

Eva and her identical twin sister, Miriam, were the only two members of her family allowed to live because they were required for a series of gruesome experiments led by the 'Angel of Death,' Dr Josef Mengele.

Fifty years after the camp was liberated, Eva returned to Auschwitz where she came face-to-face with another Nazi doctor. Kor convinced him to sign a document confirming the existence of the gas chambers and she used it as evidence against Holocaust deniers. She later forgave the Nazis for their crimes and she now preaches absolution to audiences around the world.

Eva Kor remembers the doors of the cattle car opening on to the 'separation platform' at Auschwitz-Birkenau. When she and her family got out, her parents and two older sisters were taken in one direction while she and her twin, Miriam, were taken in the other. Eva remembers looking back and seeing her mother's outstretched arms.

The twins were taken to a barracks where children were kept. She saw three bodies lying on the floor of the latrines. That night, children pointed towards the gas chambers and said, 'Look there. See the smoke and the flames? Your family must be burning there right now.'[52] Eva and Meriam never saw the rest of their family again.

The girls' lives had been spared by virtue of being twins. The notorious Nazi doctor, Josef Mengele, claimed he needed them for comparative testing to unlock the secrets of the blond-haired, blue-eyed Aryan race. Historians broadly agree that his work was of little scientific merit and it was simply an exercise in cruelty.

Eva and Miriam were separated for weeks at a time for experimentation. Eva remembers her blood being drained until she became faint. She was repeatedly injected with mystery fluids, then left for hours, naked in the 'observation lab' while her symptoms were measured and compared to her sister. After one session she got so ill, she started falling in and out of consciousness. The next morning Mengele came in and laughed as he gave her two weeks to live.

There were a total of 1,500 sets of 'Mengele Twins' at the camp, according to the Auschwitz Museum. Eva and Miriam were amongst the 200 individuals who managed to survive. Eva remembers the day they were liberated. A woman ran through the barracks shouting 'We are free! We're free! We're free!' It's a measure of the horrors the sisters endured there they were unable to discuss it with one another for decades.

Then in 1978, Eva, now settled in the United States, was watching a TV mini-series called *The Holocaust* and she began wondering what had happened to the other 'Mengele Twins.' She resolved to ask Miriam, then living in Israel, to help her track them down. They quickly found dozens of other survivors scattered around the world.

Miriam died in 1993 from a rare form of cancer, which her sister attributes to her Auschwitz injections. Eva vowed to continue the search for survivors and even returned to Auschwitz to mark the 50th anniversary of its liberation. When she arrived, she found herself standing next to Nazi doctor, Hans Münch, known as 'The Good Man of Auschwitz' because of his refusal to take part in the mass killings. He wasn't involved in the experiments but he did witness the gas chambers and Eva convinced him to sign a document confirming their existence. It was vital first-hand evidence of the mass exterminations and she used it to prove the Holocaust deniers wrong.

Kor was so grateful to Münch and his contribution that she decided to send him a card, but she couldn't find one that felt appropriate so she started writing him a letter instead. It took her four months to complete but when she sent it, it contained her forgiveness for his role in the Holocaust.

The exercise proved to be as therapeutic for Kor as it was for Münch and she tried forgiving Mengele too. To her amazement she found she could. Then in 2015, Kor travelled to Germany to give evidence at the trial of SS officer Oskar Gröning. In front of the world media, she embraced him before he was convicted of mass murder.

That image of Kor with her arms around such evil was hugely divisive. She was vilified by other Holocaust survivors who had vowed never to forgive and that was on top of the attacks she was receiving from Holocaust deniers.

A year after the Gröning trial, in 2016, CNN invited Kor to appear on a series called 'CNN Inspirations' that I was hosting in front of a studio audience.

Kor was in her early eighties by then and unable to stand unaided for long but her warmth and energy were palpable in the Green Room. She wore a black shirt, blue paisley jacket and colourful scarf. Her hair was short and reddish in colour. She had a producer and camera operator with her for a documentary she was filming which was an indication of how keen she was to get her story out. Everyone, without exception, was enamoured by her.

In the studio we took seats opposite each other on stage. Before I started the interview, I introduced a short film which showed a haunting image of Eva and Meriam amongst a group of emaciated children in striped overalls behind the barbed wire at Auschwitz. The audience watched in utter silence and by the time the film had finished we no longer saw an old lady sitting in a chair but a terrified little girl arriving at the separation platform at Auschwitz at the age of 10…

Kor: They noticed that Miriam and I looked alike and we were dressed alike and the Nazi asked my mother if we were twins and my mother didn't know what to say. She asked if that was good. The

Nazis said 'yes.' My mother said 'yes' and then she was pulled in one direction, we were pulled in the opposite direction.

Me: That was the last time you saw her?

Kor: Yes. That was 72 years ago in May.

Me: And still as clear today as it was then?

Kor: Very, very clear and I go back to Auschwitz every year and the focal point of my story starts at the selection platform where I saw my parents and my family for the last time.

Me: It's unimaginable…

Kor: Within 30 minutes, we were separated and never to see them again.

Me: And that, on its own, obviously would traumatize anyone. People have families and they can relate to that perhaps but they can't relate to what happened to you afterwards. Why were they interested in you as a twin and what did they do to you?

Kor: They wanted to discover the secret to fertility. They wanted to increase the Aryan race and what Hitler wanted was for every German mother to have not one child but two, three or more. They also used us for medical experiments that, for instance, in my case, I was injected with a deadly germ. And Mengele and stood by my bed…

Me: The famous doctor…

Kor: …right, and said I only had two weeks to live. As I learned years later, through the Auschwitz Museum, would I have died, Miriam would have been killed by an injection to the heart and then Mengele would have done the comparative autopsies, my diseased organs, comparing them to hers. So also they wanted to know how germs worked. In normal life you cannot do that, but in Auschwitz they could do anything.

Me: Eventually you were saved, incredibly, after this horrendous experience and you settled in the United States but you wanted to get back in touch with the twins there, the other twins. Very few of them left of course, but tell us how you did that…

Kor: Well I didn't know how to find the children in 1978 when I began dealing with my story. I only had the images in my mind and I knew that there were some who survived. So, I began a six year effort in trying to locate those little children, who were now grown-ups of course, without any names or addresses. I really appealed to the media to help me. We got a front-page story in one of the Israeli papers and that started the flood of information. In one week my sister located, with the help of that story in Israel, 80 surviving individuals of the experiments living in 10 countries in four continents.

Me: So, you were finally able to speak to people who could relate to your experience.

Kor: Right.

Me: But that wasn't enough for you. You want to reach the Nazis; you wanted to speak to the Nazis. Why did you want to do that?

Kor: Well that happened much later, about ten years later. I met, at my own initiative, with a Nazi doctor, hoping that I could learn some of the things that happened in Auschwitz. He did not know anything about our experiment but an idea popped in to my head and I asked him if he knew anything about the gas chambers. And when he described it, he was actually signing the death certificates as people were dying. The number of people, I never heard about it and I asked him to go with me to Auschwitz to sign a document that the gas chambers existed, at the ruins.

Me: Why was that so important to you?

Kor: Well unfortunately there are people in the world who say the Holocaust didn't happen and they say the Jews invented that story. So, it was important for me that it was a Nazi that was willing to document the facts. And he was willing to go with me to Auschwitz and sign a document about what he told me, what happened in the gas chambers. I felt that it was a very important and brave thing on his part.

Me: So instead of hating him, you ended up thanking him because he gave you something that you wanted, you wanted the world to understand.

Kor: Well I wanted to thank him for his willingness to document the gas chambers, because that to me was an important fact. And because I didn't know how to thank him, I fortunately came up with a gift of forgiving him. That was my gift to him, but it became a gift to me too.

Me: Because you finally had control over something in your life.

Kor: I was finally free from what happened in Auschwitz. Emotionally, I was in charge of my own feelings and all victims in the world can relate to that; that while the tragedy is long gone, the pain lingers on and nobody can heal that pain except each one of us can do it for ourselves.[53]

At that point I handed over to a colleague in the audience and as I did so I saw tears in people's eyes. I had been so engrossed in to the interview I wasn't aware of how deeply the people around me had been affected.

A young woman wanted to know why Kor forgave the Nazis. It had already been explained but it was so much to take in.

'Why forgive? Why not hate?' I asked Kor, 'Well, I never really hated them, I just didn't like them. Hate is a very strong emotion and it is actually hurting the victim more than the perpetrator. Forgiveness gave me the power to do something that they could never change and it healed me because, then, I was no longer angry. I could go on with my life without carrying that baggage of pain with me.'[54]

It was amazing to see such an old, frail lady command such a large space without lifting a finger, literally. She's hardly moved, which shows the power of authentic voice. Her experience was hard enough to comprehend, let alone how she survived and then managed to find her peace.

I had asked Kor before the interview how she thinks she connects with audiences and she told me, 'I am connecting on the human level that we all have problems in our lives and we have been wronged or all feel like we have been wronged and so hurt so there are wounds that we want to heal and only we can heal them. Nobody else can. I cannot forgive for anybody else's problem. It's not going to help them. I can only forgive in my own name, for my own pain, and the forgiveness is a proactive act rather than just letting go. Because forgiveness is very empowering,' she said pointing to her cause.

Kor was leading by example, showing that if *she* was able to forgive, then you certainly should be able to and perhaps you owed it to her to try.

Give it a go now, as you read this. Think about that person who's hurt you. Now try letting it go. You'll feel the cloud starting to lift … you're reclaiming all that energy you've wasted on someone who doesn't deserve it.

Kor's story plays in to many conversations but ultimately it's a journey to inner peace. She shows how you can get there with a simple act of forgiveness, whatever you've been through. Her credibility to lead that conversation is undeniable as is her strength of character, but it's the magnitude of what she's addressing that gives her so much clout. A simple mental trick, that changes lives. Her gift to you. I saw the effects of that in the audience that day. She cuts wide but she also cuts deep and once you've heard her tell her story, it never leaves you, not because of the horror but because of the hope. Her clout is rooted in the scale of the conversation she's addressing.

Kor's Cloutfile

Cause: Forgiveness.

Credibility: Overcame unimaginable pain and speaks to it eloquently.

Character: Honest about what happened to her and consistent in why she's willing to talk about it.

Conversation: Finding your inner peace.

Connection: If she can forgive, so can you.

Cachet: As a survivor of Auschwitz she had an unassailable right to be heard and chance to lead the conversation.

CHAPTER 5

DONALD TRUMP
CONNECTION

*'The media and establishment want me out of
the race so badly – I WILL NEVER DROP OUT
OF THE RACE, WILL NEVER LET MY SUP-
PORTERS DOWN! #MAGA'.*
Donald Trump, Twitter, 8 October 2016.[55]

Born 14 June 1946 in Queens, New York, Donald
John Trump was the fourth child of real estate tycoon
Fred Trump. After misbehaving at school, he was sent to
military academy at the age of 13 and went on to graduate from the prestigious Wharton business school at the
University of Pennsylvania. His father loaned him $1m
to start a real estate business and later handed over control of the entire family business. Donald diversified out
of residential units into hotels, casinos and skyscrapers.
He also bought in to the Miss Universe and Miss USA
beauty pageants, he starred in *The Apprentice* reality TV
series and co-authored several books including *The Art
of the Deal*.

His brother, Fred, died in 1981 following a long battle with alcoholism after which Donald vowed never to touch a drink again.[56] He has been married three times, has five children and famously beat Democratic candidate Hillary Clinton to become the 45th President of the United States of America.

It was July 2015 and I was waiting for Donald Trump to arrive at his magnificent and historic golf resort at Turnberry, Scotland or 'Trump Turnberry' as he'd rebranded it. I was looking out of a window from the hotel, perched high above the legendary course, out to the sea. The rugged, blustery west coast of the country is a sight to behold whatever the weather but on a crisp, sunny day, it's nothing less than awe-inspiring.

Trump was already a big name at the time but not the level that we know him now. He was a property mogul and reality TV star who had announced his run for President the month before. His headline policy was a wall he wanted to build along the border with Mexico to prevent illegal migrants from crossing into the United States.

'When Mexico sends its people, they're not sending their best,' he'd said. 'They're sending people that have lots of problems, and they're bringing those problems to us. They're bringing drugs. They're bringing crime. They're rapists. And some, I assume, are good people.'[57]

It's fair to say most British journalists at the time didn't take his bid for office seriously but many had flocked to Turnberry to cover his visit anyway because he was doing surprisingly well in the polls.

There was a commotion in the lobby and I went outside to see the Trump chopper come in to land. He was swamped by cameras and reporters as he stepped off, delivered a few cursory remarks and then continued up the steps to the hotel.

Later, he held a press conference, where he took us through a lengthy presentation about his plans to redevelop the hotel. The project was being overseen by his son Eric, whom he introduced from the back. When Trump opened it up for questions the discussion turned quickly to politics however.

One reporter started asking about the level of diplomacy required to be President but Trump interrupted saying, 'I don't think so, no. I think there's been too much diplomacy. I think there's been too much. I think we're so politically correct in our country that people are sick and tired of it and things aren't getting done. Certainly, you need to be diplomatic. I mean we're diplomatic in our country and everybody hates us all over the world. We're politically correct and the world hates the United States, if you look at it. The world takes advantage of the United States on trade, on just about everything. We're so nice, they're nice, they're as you say politically correct and yet we've never been more unpopular, and it's probably almost never been a more dangerous time.'[58]

His answers were rambling but frank and it was actually quite refreshing to hear a politician answer the questions put to them.

A few of us hung around afterwards in the hope of getting a one-on-one interview but the hotel PR told us it was unlikely and the others dropped away. I decided to take a risk and stay overnight in case he changed his mind. If I got this, it would be a big scoop, if I didn't my bosses would justifiably question the added expense. The PR said she would keep trying Trump on my behalf but she didn't appear to have direct access to him, instead she was having to go through his head of security instead which speaks to the level of control Trump has over his own publicity.

In the meantime, I was introduced to Eric who talked me through the hotel redevelopment plans but I had to be honest with him and say it wasn't going to make it to air on CNN.

The next morning, I had a magnificent Scottish breakfast in the dining room overlooking the sea and retired back to the lobby to digest it in one of the plush armchairs. Life on the road isn't normally this leisurely or luxurious in the news business but I was there for one reason and had very little control over him.

I had been waiting more than a day now and still no indication of whether Trump would change his mind and speak to me. As the time ticked away, it was becoming increasingly difficult for me to justify the trip and I started to worry that I wasn't going to get anything and would have to go back to London with my tail between my legs.

I saw Trump coming down the grand wooden staircase in his golfing gear and I entertained the idea of approaching him myself but experience had taught me that it's a tactic that can often backfire. He needed to make his own call on it. As he reached the bottom step, he was enveloped by his entourage. I pretended not to watch but could see his red 'Make America Great Again' cap bobbing around in the corner of my eye. Then I felt it coming towards me and, before I knew it, he was leaning over my armchair. 'I hear you've been waiting to speak to me.'

'Er, yes,' I replied, standing up to shake his hand.

'Let's go outside,' he said and walked off expecting me to follow, which of course I did but not before I'd helped the cameraman gather up his equipment.

When I caught up with Trump, he asked me whilst still walking: 'Do you know Jeff Zucker?' (the President of CNN)

'Yes, I do,' I replied.

'I know Jeff,' he said, but he stopped there which was intriguing.

Had he just sent me a warning shot? If so, it backfired because now I had to assert my independence even more to make sure I couldn't be accused of giving him an easy ride in the interview.

He told me he didn't have long so I suggested the cameraman record the interview 'off-the-shoulder' rather than setting up the tripod. As I did so, Trump positioned himself strategically with the golf course in the back of his shot. I let it go because it was a wonderful setting and it spoke to where we were.

I began by asking him about the golf course to settle him in then moved on to foreign policy, which is what I really wanted to explore with him. I asked about the annexation of Crimea by Russia which he described as 'Europe's problem.' He made it clear that President Putin would respect him though.[59] 'My whole thing is Make America Great Again. You can't get simpler than that.'

Then on to immigration…

Trump: I turned out to be right. Excuse me; many people have agreed that I was right.

Me: About rapists? Do they think you were right about that?

Trump: Right, do me a favour. You are now doing like everybody else does OK and what I said was that Mexico is sending and that's true. Mexico is sending, people are coming through that border from all over the world they are coming through the border. We have a porous border. We have a border where you can just walk right in to the country. And you can't do that. To have a country you have to have a strong border. You have to have a really strong border and this has to stop. What's going on now has to stop.

Me: Who will build the wall and how will it be made?

Trump: I will build the wall and Mexico is going to pay for it and they will be happy to pay for it because Mexico is making so much money from the United States that that's going to be peanuts and all these characters say: 'Oh they won't pay.' They won't pay because they don't know the first thing about how to negotiate. Trust me, Mexico will pay for it. Thank you very much.[60]

And with that he ended the interview, walking back inside. On the way, he called out sarcastically, 'I hope you get a raise!'

He was clearly unhappy with how the interview had gone for him but he gave as good as he got and I thought he actually handled it pretty well.

Myself and the team went to edit the interview and it played out over the course of the day on CNN.

That evening, satisfied with a good day's work, we retired to the fancy whisky bar and I met up with the hotel PR to thank her. Before long, Trump arrived and rather alarmingly made his way over to us. I braced for an outburst but instead I got, 'Great interview! I thought it was very fair.'

It was odd, but intriguing at the same time so I went with it. It got even more surreal when he started addressing the PR as if she worked for me. I let her slip away when she saw the opportunity and I was left on my own with Trump.

'People are fascinated by how well your campaign is going,' I told him. Then I realised he didn't have his cap on any more and I became fixated with his hair. It was much thicker than I imagined – wispy, yet immobile.

'You're based in London?' he asked.

'Yes,' I replied. 'I've been covering the election here. It was all about immigration and whether or not we should leave the European Union.'

'Really..?' he asked, indicating he wanted to hear more.

I explained how Nigel Farage from the UK Independence Party had emerged as the star of the campaign with his anti-EU rhetoric. Trump seemed fascinated, as if it was the first time he was hearing it, though perhaps he was being coy. He took me over to meet speak to Eric and wife Lara. She told me she worked in TV too and we discussed her role on the show *Inside Edition*.

Trump left and came back with his son-in-law Jared Kushner who was pristinely dressed in crisp new golfing gear. 'I have media interests in the US,' he told me, 'The New York Observer.' We talked a bit about the digitalisation of media and how the lines were being blurred between print and TV. He wasn't officially part of the Trump campaign at that point. I went back over my analysis of the UK election with him and he seemed interested, though he also had a quizzical look on his face – the one I use myself in meetings when I want to look engaged but don't want to speak.

I realised before long that I was the only person in the bar who had a drink in his hand and it was getting late so I said my goodbyes and headed to my room. On the way I remember thinking to myself what a nice family unit they appeared to be. Politics aside, Kushner seemed focused and sophisticated, Eric and Lara were open and friendly and Trump gave the impression of being a proud family man.

Did he introduce me to Eric and Jared so they could test whether I was worth cultivating? Perhaps, but I haven't heard from any of them since.

A couple of years later, I was having dinner with a Washington insider and when I described my encounter with Trump, I was told he was 'transactional.' He did the interview 'because he wanted international publicity for his golf course and he was using Jeff (Zucker) as leverage.'

I wasn't sure it was as simple as that. I felt Trump operated on a particularly personal level and I could see how he could be convincing for people who shared his world view.

When Trump approached me in the hotel lobby, he didn't say much but with the few words that he did use, he showed empathy for how long I had been waiting then took me outside for an interview. That's the essence of how to connect with anybody in my experience. You identify how they feel, articulate it and then offer a solution.

You can apply the same analysis to his plan to build the wall. He said people were right to fear illegal immigrants. They were 'stealing' American jobs and importing crime.

He then offered to build the wall to make them feel safe again. He said Americans were right to feel angry too with government for failing to do anything about it. He promised to 'drain the swamp' in Washington and Trump fans liked the phrase so much, they started chanting it at his rallies, as they did 'Build the wall! Build the wall!'

When Trump got that type of feedback he knew he was on to something and he ramped up the rhetoric even more, even using profanities which was unheard of on the presidential campaign trail. His 'base' didn't care, they had lost faith in traditional politics anyway. It was all highly connective for them.

What's extraordinary is how Trump managed to relate to people he appeared to have nothing in common with. Take the white, rural, disenfranchised worker that commentators often pointed to as his typical supporter. What did they have in common with a billionaire property magnate and TV star from Manhattan?

I'll let him explain. Here's an extract from the first speech of his campaign, delivered in the glittering Trump Tower in June 2015, as he announced his run for president:

'I started off in a small office with my father in Brooklyn and Queens, and my father said, and I love my father – I learned so much, he was a great negotiator. I learned so much just sitting at his feet playing with blocks listening to him negotiate with subcontractors. But I learned a lot. But he used to say, "Donald, don't go into Manhattan. That's the big leagues. We don't know anything about that. Don't do it."

I said, "I gotta go into Manhattan. I gotta build those big buildings. I gotta do it, Dad. I've gotta do it." And after four or five years in Brooklyn, I ventured into Manhattan and did a lot of great deals, the Grand Hyatt Hotel. I was responsible for the convention center on the west side. I did a lot of great deals, and I did them early and young, and now I'm building all over the world, and I love what I'm doing.'[61]

For that disenfranchised worker, struggling to find work, Trump sounded like a winner and someone they could identify with because they wanted to live the same American dream. He was appealing to their hopes and showing how anything's possible. Manhattan is where he made it, not where he was from – that was Queens.

Then he explained how he was going to help them follow in his path. 'I will be the greatest jobs president that God ever created. I tell you that. I'll bring back our jobs from China, from Mexico, from Japan, from so many places. I'll bring back our jobs, and I'll bring back our money.'

That's exactly what they wanted to hear and Trump repeated the jobs mantra throughout his campaign with great success. He argued he was uniquely qualified, from his years in business, to renegotiate the 'disastrous' trade deals that had bled the economy dry.

By casting himself as an underdog, Trump not only made himself more relatable but it also allowed him to distance himself from the 'ruling elites' who, according to his narrative, had trashed the country. I think he genuinely believed it too because it would explain his constant self-validation. 'Let me tell you, I'm a really smart guy.'

(*ABC*, March 2011[62]). 'Sorry losers and haters, but my I.Q. is one of the highest – and you all know it!' (*Twitter*, 2013[63]). 'I went to the Wharton School of Finance; I'm, like, a really smart person' (Phoenix rally, July 2015[64]).

Trump wasn't the first politician to use the underdog plotline but he was the most effective because of his experience in reality TV which is built on the narrative. It's the undiscovered talent that finally breaks through; David vs Goliath; the one against the many. Trump's take was the political outsider taking on the ruling elite, as illustrated by the script from his last TV ad of his campaign:

'Our movement is about replacing a failed and corrupt political establishment with a new government controlled by you, the American people. The establishment has trillions of dollars at stake in this election. For those who control the levers of power in Washington and for the global special interests, they partner with these people that don't have your good in mind. The political establishment, that is trying to stop us, is the same group responsible for our disastrous trade deals, massive illegal immigration, and economic and foreign policies that have bled our country dry. The political establishment has brought about the destruction of our factories and our jobs as they flee to Mexico, China, and other countries all around the world. It's a global power structure that is responsible for the economic decisions that have robbed our working class, stripped our country of its wealth, and put that money into the pockets of a handful of large corporations and political entities. The only thing that can stop this corrupt machine is you. The only force strong enough to save our country is us. The only people brave enough to vote out this corrupt establishment is you, the American people. I'm doing this for the people and for the movement and we will take back this country for you and we will make America great again.'[65]

It was an apocalyptic vision. He portrayed himself as the only person that could save the country from its perilous state. All he needed was your support. It's the language of populist revolt and he rode it all the way to the White House.

Every underdog needs a nemesis and Trump's 'global power structure' is particularly abstract but it allowed him to roll anyone and anything that got in his way in to one all-encompassing enemy. Politicians, bankers, international institutions, even his own party leadership were fair game, as were the news media whose very reason for being is to speak truth unto power. 'If the disgusting and corrupt media covered me honestly and didn't put false meaning into the words I say, I would be beating Hillary by 20%,' Trump tweeted in August 2016.[66]

It was Hillary Clinton who bore the brunt of the attacks as his main opponent. She epitomised the ruling class for him, out to serve nothing but her own self-interest. Her biggest vulnerability was the 'character issue' that kept showing up in the polls and that's where Trump went in for the kill.

When Clinton said, rightly, that she had done nothing illegal when she used a private email account for official business as Secretary of State, he branded her 'Crooked Hillary' anyway. That's because he knew people cared less about the legality of what she did and more about the sense of entitlement that came with going around the official email system. That played right in to Trump's narrative.

'Lock her up! Lock her up!' they started chanting at the rallies, confirming to Trump and that was on to another winner.

When the infamous *Access Hollywood* came out, I was one of those who thought I must be terminal for Trump but I was wrong. We heard him on a bus talking about how he tried to f*** a married woman and then brag about groping women.[67] He issued a rare public apology, but in the same breath he dragged up historic allegations against Bill Clinton.

'Bill Clinton has actually abused women and Hillary has bullied, attacked, shamed and intimidated his victims.' Trump claimed.[68] In other words, if he was going down, Clinton was going down with him so she couldn't use the tape to get an advantage over him in the race. It was a brutal tactic but it wasn't out of character and didn't undermine his cause or 'movement' either. It may have even strengthened his connection with certain elements of his audience.

Wherever he saw weakness, Trump exploited it – at rallies, on TV and on digital. Shortly before the election, *Bloomberg Businessweek*, published an interview with Trump's digital media director, Brad Parscale, who explained how they were using a comment Clinton had made two decades before against her, about 'super predators' and African American males.

'On Oct. 24, Trump's team began placing spots on select African American radio stations,' Joshua Green and Sasha Issenberg wrote for Bloomberg.

'In San Antonio, a young staffer showed off a South Park-style animation he'd created of Clinton delivering the "super predator" line (using audio from her original 1996 sound bite), as cartoon text popped up around her: "Hillary Thinks African Americans are Super Predators." The animation will be delivered to certain African American voters through Facebook "dark posts" – nonpublic posts whose viewership the campaign controls so that, as Parscale puts it, "only the people we want to see it, see it." The aim is to depress Clinton's vote total. "We know because we've modeled this," says the official. "It will dramatically affect her ability to turn these people out."[69]

The African American turnout was all-important for Clinton and it was indeed down in the previous election,[70] only by 1% but every vote counted on this one. Trump's win was razor thin in the end. Three states did it for him – Michigan, Wisconsin and Pennsylvania – where he had a combined lead of only about 80,000 votes.[71]

We will never know exactly to what extent Russian meddling, fake news and/or data harvesting helped Trump but ultimately Clinton didn't connect with enough people in the right places to beat him. She ended up with more votes overall so she didn't lack clout but Trump targeted more effectively.

According to Michael Wolff's insider story *Fire and Fury* Trump surprised even himself by coming out in front. 'As the campaign came to an end, Trump himself was sanguine,' writes Wolff. 'His ultimate goal, after all, had never been to win. "I can be the most famous man in the world," he had told his aide Sam Nunberg at the outset of the race.'

Wolff suggests Trump wanted to use the campaign to raise his profile enough to launch 'Trump TV.' If true, that gives interesting context to an interview Jared Kushner gave after the election.

'We weren't afraid to fail,' Kushner tells Forbes in November 2016. 'We tried to do things very cheaply, very quickly. And if it wasn't working, we would kill it quickly.'[72]

In other words, if a message wasn't working they would drop it and focus on the ones that did. It was an extension of what Trump was doing at his rallies when he ramped up the messages that received the biggest response.

'It meant making quick decisions, fixing things that were broken and scaling things that worked,' says Kushner. He had teams of data scientists scouting out any shifts in sentiment they could respond to.

If you're not intending to win, you can have that strategy because you don't have to worry about the living up to the promises you are make.

During his campaign, Trump famously said, 'I could stand in the middle of 5th Avenue and shoot somebody and I wouldn't lose voters.'[73] That shows how connected he felt with his audience.

For the purposes of this book, I have only focussed on Trump's rise to the White House and how he developed enough clout to become the most powerful person in the world. Whatever your view of him, we can all learn from how he did that, despite his complete lack of political experience.

The true test of his clout would only come once he made office. Could he live up to the promises he made on the campaign trail? Was he really going to build the wall and make Mexico pay for it?

Clout is hard won and easily lost, particularly in the White House, and history will need to be his judge.

Trump's Campaign Cloutfile

Cause: 'Make America Great Again'.

Credibility: 'Self-made' billionaire businessman and proven deal-maker.

Character: Uncompromised, unfiltered underdog.

Conversation: How to make American great again.

Connection: He expressed the fears of voters and promising to resolve them.

Cachet: The most talked-about man in the world.

CHAPTER 6

HM QUEEN ELIZABETH II CACHET

'In the end, probably, the training is the answer to a great many things. You can do a lot if you're properly trained. I hope I have been.'
The Queen, 'Elizabeth R', BBC, 1992.[74]

QUEEN ELIZABETH IS THE LONGEST serving monarch in British history. Born in 1926, she was home schooled and aged 18 she joined the war effort, eventually qualifying as a military driver. She married Prince Philip of Denmark and Greece in 1947 and acceded to the throne in 1952 when Winston Churchill was Prime Minister and Harry Truman was in the White House.

Of her four children, Charles is the eldest and is her heir apparent. Princes William and then George follow in the line of succession.

The Queen's primary role is as UK Head of State but she holds numerous other official positions, most notably as Head of The Commonwealth, Supreme Governor of the Church of England and Head of Nation.

She has travelled widely and holds hundreds of patronages for a wide range of charities and organisations. She has a passion for horses and dogs.

The first big news event I can recall clearly as a child is the marriage of Prince Charles to Lady Diana Spencer in 1981. I was 9, and I remember walking up the lane to a neighbour's house with my family to a viewing party. I can still see the mums nestled into the big leather sofas, telling us to quieten down. Big royal events are one of the few occasions when Britons, particularly the English, feel a sense of patriotism.

I also remember where I was 16 years later, when I heard Diana had been killed in a car crash. It was in the early hours of the morning and I was still up with friends from a birthday party the night before. Someone had been out to buy a packet of cigarettes and heard the news on a radio in the store. None of us could quite take it in; it was as if someone we knew personally had died when none of us had never even met her.

Over the next few days, that sense of grief consumed the entire country. I was in London so I went to Diana's home at Kensington Palace to view the sea of flowers I had seen reported on the news. It was more overwhelming than I had imagined. Bouquet laid carefully against bouquet until they stretched out into the park from the palace gates. People were standing, staring, some kneeling to read the cards, others just hugging in consolation. Men as well as women. Britons aren't very good at expressing themselves in public but it was as if all those inhibitions had been stripped away and everyone had just collapsed in an emotional heap.

A few days later, I watched the funeral broadcast live on TV. The image that haunts so many of us is of the teenaged William and Harry walking, heads bowed behind their mother's coffin. Who couldn't empathise with them? There was much talk of the silence that descended on London that day but Harry remembers it differently. 'Of course there was a huge amount of silence, but what I remember is every 50 yards or whatever, certain people in the crowd just unable to contain their emotion. That was a big thing.'[75]

Inside Westminster Abbey, the boys were afforded more privacy, with the broadcasters agreeing not to show their faces during the service. An estimated 31 million viewers tuned in to watch the service and that was just in the UK.[76] It still stands as the most watched live TV event in British history.

Diana's brother, Charles, famously lashed out at the media in his eulogy saying, 'a girl given the name of the ancient goddess of hunting was, in the end, the most hunted person of the modern age.'

Another poignant moment people remember was Elton John's rendition of 'Candle in the Wind' which he had re-written for Diana. It hit such a nerve that it went on to become the best-selling single of all time in the UK and US.[77]

A decade later, when the BBC surveyed Britons about their most memorable public events, the death of Diana came second only to the 9/11 terror attacks in New York.[78] People remember where they were and who they were with when they heard the news. There is surely no other family in western culture that is associated as many 'flashbulb memories' as the British royals. It's not just their personal stories that pepper a thousand years of history but also their presence at countless momentous events.

Diana's clout was unquestionable. The Prime Minister Tony Blair put his finger on it when he called her 'The People's Princess'[79] upon her death. She was part of conversations about fashion, celebrity activism and family breakdown but it was her contribution to the debate around royalty that made her famous in the first place, and for a while she controlled that which is where she gained particular cachet.

In the aftermath of her death, the tabloid newspapers picked up on how the flag over Buckingham Palace hadn't been lowered in respect for Diana. They then questioned why The Queen hadn't returned to the capital from her holiday on the Balmoral Estate in Scotland.

'The people are suffering. Speak to us Ma'am,' headlined the Mirror with two images of a woman and a boy, both kneeling with their hands to their faces in grief. The Daily Express had a picture of The Queen looking steely-faced – 'Show us you care,' read the banner. The Sun's front page simply asked, 'Where is our Queen? Where is her flag?'[80]

Elizabeth has a natural gauge for public opinion and she hadn't lost sense of that but William and Harry were staying with her along with their father, Prince Charles, and she had simply put her duty to them above that of the country. Nobody could remember her ever doing that which is what many struggled with.

'My grandmother wanted to protect her two grandsons and my father as well,' William told a documentary team in 2017.[81] 'Our grandmother deliberately removed the newspapers and things like that, so there was nothing in the house at all. So, we didn't know what was going on.' William says he was thankful for 'the privacy to mourn, to collect our thoughts, and to just have that space away from everybody.'

The flag was a separate issue of protocol. It had never been lowered, not even upon the death of a monarch but, on Blair's advice, The Queen did cut her holiday short by a day and returned to London with the boys to view the flowers outside Buckingham Palace before going inside to pay a glowing tribute to Diana on live TV.

For the funeral, The Queen broke with protocol and had the flag lowered. She also gave her approval for the royal standard to be draped over Diana's coffin, even though she wasn't officially a member of the royal family when she died.

Blair recalls, 'There was going to be a risk that the country's sense of loss turned to a sense of anger and grievance, and then turned against the monarchy.'[82] The Queen had lost control of the national conversation and there was a price to her cachet. Rightly or wrongly, people felt let down. They'd grown accustomed to seeing her appear in times of crisis and she wasn't there for them. She had her reasons to stay away of course but perhaps even she hadn't realised how ingrained she had become in the national conscience. The Monarchy's approval ratings probably didn't bounce back properly until Prince William's blockbuster marriage to Kate Middleton in 2011.

A monarch is ultimately judged on whether they strengthen or weaken The Crown and when you consider the challenges Elizabeth has overcome during the course of her long reign she may well go down as one of the greatest in British history.

The world was a different place when Elizabeth took to the throne, at the age of 25. An opinion poll in 1956 found that 35 per cent of Britons thought she had been appointed by god.[83] Nobody questioned her right to rule, but she never took that for granted either.

As a princess, she delivered a speech in Cape Town, South Africa to mark her 21st birthday and it still defines her monarchy. 'I declare before you all that my whole life, whether it be long or short, shall be devoted to your service and the service of our great imperial family to which we all belong,' she famously said.[84]

That commitment to lifelong service is often cited as the reason that she never abdicated. The more ambitious promise she made though was to 'the great imperial family,' or British Empire. This was 1947, the year India declared independence, prompting a domino effect across the 'colonies.' Nation after nation peeled away and seized control back from London.

By the time Elizabeth was Queen, the empire was in freefall and she had to find a way to reinvent herself or go down in history as the monarch who squandered what her forbearers had spent a millennium building up for her.

She spotted her opportunity when the countries leaving the empire regrouped under an association that we now know as The Commonwealth. The Queen inherited her role as its Head but elevated it to a core responsibility. It meant that when countries left one side of her portfolio (the empire) they rejoined another (the Commonwealth). She was able therefore to keep her commitment to the imperial family and retain her international footprint.

When she became Queen, The Commonwealth had 8 members and, at the last count, it had 53[85] with a combined population of 2.4 billion people.[86] It's nearly six times the size the empire ever was and new members have joined that were never even colonised by the UK.

'Over many years you have been the Commonwealth's most steadfast and fervent champion,' Prime Minister Theresa May noted in a speech at Buckingham Palace in April 2018 in the presence of Her Majesty during the Commonwealth Heads of Government Meeting (CHOGM).

Elizabeth always prioritised the biennial CHOGM meetings and this one had particular poignancy because it was set to be her last as she cut back on travel. She has visited all but two Commonwealth countries, many repeatedly and may have even stemmed the tide of re-publicanism itself, with 15 countries including Canada, Jamaica and Australia choosing to retain her as head of state even as they went independent.

A telling tweet was sent out by the Australian Prime Minister, Malcolm Turnball, in July 2017 after he had been received by The Queen at Buckingham Palace: 'Al-though I am a Republican, I am also an Elizabethan. It was an honour to meet Her Majesty today at Buckingham Palace.'[87]

Turnball was co-founder of the Australian Republican Movement but he also knew that removing The Queen could be political suicide due to the clout she wields personally in his home country.

One of the few people in the world who can relate to Elizabeth's position is that other long-serving and revered European Queen, Margrethe II of Denmark. I inter-viewed her in Copenhagen in 2012 to mark her 40th year on the throne and we spoke about the shifting sentiments towards monarchy during her reign, in particular the loss of deference in Western society.

Queen Margrethe: I suppose we are not taken for granted the way one was in those days. The monarchy was taken more or less for granted, unless you were dead against it of course. You have to be conscious of the fact that nothing can be taken for granted like that today; in fact, you never should take that sort of thing for granted.

Me: Your position?

Queen Margrethe: Basically, you don't work to keep a position; you work to keep your country. You give your life to your country when you become a head of a country.

I remember quite well listening to Princess Elizabeth's speech which was broadcast around her birthday when she was 21. That was 1947. I seem to remember having listened to that speech – the way she dedicated her life to the country – and that was an example that I very much felt, when I grew older. That was what it was about.[88]

That 21st birthday message by Elizabeth was broadcast around the world on radio but she also recorded it for the emerging medium of television and that's the image that sticks in many people's minds. You saw a youthful princess with the gravitas and vision of a stateswoman-in-waiting. People knew she was going to be a leader but now they felt it too.

Elizabeth consistently embraced new media as she reached out to the widest possible audience. She opened official Facebook and Twitter accounts before any of her grandchildren. She inadvertently invented event television too when she allowed live cameras in to her coronation at Westminster Abbey in 1953. People went out and bought TV's just to watch it. *The Times of London* wrote, 'By penetrating at last, even vicariously, into the solemn mysteriousness of the Abbey scene, multitudes who had hoped merely to see for themselves the splendour and the pomp, found themselves comprehending for the first time the true nature of the occasion.'

When colour television came along, The Queen invited that in too, by granting extraordinary access to the film-maker Richard Cawston for a fly-on-the-wall documentary called 'Royal Family' in 1969. 37 million people tuned in to watch The Queen and Duke of Edinburgh barbequing sausages at Balmoral Castle in Scotland. 'Are the sandwiches ready?' she asks.

Historian Andrew Rosen noted how this early landmark in reality TV consciously blurred the distinction between the public functions and private lives of the royal family, 'thus the daylight began to intrude upon magic.'[89]

The film aired twice and hasn't been shown in full since. Perhaps it was the moment Elizabeth realised you can allow the media too much access and that there is value in retaining some privacy and mystique.

The Queen has never gone as far as granting a formal sit-down interview, though she has been recorded 'in conversation' discussing subjects unlikely to cause offence, such as her coronation or her love of trees. The reason they can't be classed interviews is that she leads the interaction. Despite modernisation, the monarch still speaks first.

Elizabeth does, on occasion, express herself on more serious matters but you can count the number of times she's done that on one hand, and it's never on camera. In 2014, ahead of the referendum on Scottish independence, she spoke to a well-wisher outside church knowing that reporters were standing by to follow up with anyone she spoke to. There were rumours at the time that she was concerned that Scots might vote to separate from the United Kingdom and, in that context, she told the well-wisher she hoped 'people will think very carefully about the future.'[90] The comments were picked up by Scottish media and perhaps it did help swing the vote towards a 'no' to independence. The polls showed many Scots were undecided at the time.

Generally speaking, we have no idea what The Queen thinks which prompts the question, how does she manage to connect with such a broad audience without ever expressing how she feels?

Imagine she's out on a public engagement and is being shown around a new skyscraper. You know she cares enough about the building to accept the invitation but you don't know whether she likes skyscrapers or not. What you see is someone familiar failing to show any emotion but our natural instinct is to fill that void with our own way of thinking – we project our feelings on to her. If you like skyscrapers, you therefore assume she does too. If you don't, then you sense that she shares the same view. It's like looking in to a mirror. She's managing to empathise and connect with you at the same time as everyone else. That's what gives her such universal appeal.

On the occasions she has let herself go in public, a tear at a memorial service for example, she's expressed the majority view which only adds to her appeal.

The Queen's ability to avoid controversy has earned her respect at every level. I was in Normandy, France with her for the D-Day war commemorations in July 2014 and saw how world leaders deferred to her. She was the longest serving head of state which brings with it a certain reverence but there's also a respect there for the way she's inhabited the position.

As the leaders came together for the requisite 'family photo,' a space was reserved for her in the centre of the shot next to host Francois Hollande. After the picture was taken, President Obama escorted her down the steps as if he were a member of her staff and President Putin of Russia allowed them to go ahead. Yes, they were both probably acting on their gentlemanly instincts but it also felt like an acknowledgement of The Queen's personal status. She's been at the centre of so many conversations for such a long period of time, it's hard to imagine a world without her and it all adds to her rare cachet.

'The Queen has been in my life longer than any other person apart from my elder sister,' notes actress Helen Mirren,[91] who has studied Elizabeth closely for her portrayals of the monarch on stage and screen. That omnipresence explains why it's so unsettling for people when The Queen doesn't appear when she's expected, such as after Diana's death or when she missed a regular church appearance on Christmas Day in 2016. All we were told that time was that she had a cold, but speculation soon mounted that it could be more serious, not helped by a vacuum of information from the palace.

When The Queen failed to appear again at the New Year service, newsrooms around the world started deploying teams to Buckingham Palace. It really was just a cold but the over-reaction illustrates the towering presence The Queen has in the public consciousness.

Monarchy isn't a system anyone would recreate now in a major western liberal democracy but people don't seem ready to let go of it either, at home or abroad.

In Australia where The Queen is still Head of State, I've come across many republicans in the crowds of well-wishers during official royal tours. They are able to detach the celebrity of royalty from the institution itself though. You can have Prince William as your pin-up without wanting him to be King.

I detected a similar sentiment in the republican stronghold of Quebec but in other parts of Canada there was more deference to the monarchy. The Queen speaks to the history of the country and there's a certain pride perhaps in having something that their southern neighbours in the US are often so fascinated by.

In America, royal well-wishers tend to come in pairs, mothers and daughters, keen to catch a glimpse of a real-life prince and princess. Hollywood can take much of the credit for that. Diana was the embodiment of a Disney princess, just as Kate Middleton and Meghan Markle were after her. Anyone can be President but you can't be a King or Queen without being born to royalty, or marrying in. It's the unattainability of that status draws such fascination. They're almost mystical figures. Wherever I am in the world and I speak to a member of the public after they have met a royal, their most common response is: 'They're so normal!' As if they aren't real until you actually come face-to-face with one.

That's why Meghan Markle is such a star. She *was* normal and now she isn't. She's part of the fantasy. If you look into her trolls online many just come across as jealous.

Many appear to be supportive of Markle and what she represents. On the day her engagement to Harry was announced, an African American collcague told me she couldn't believe someone like Markle had 'penetrated' the royal family. The same excitement came through on the Facebook feed of an edition of my show 'CNN Talk' that I anchored from Buckingham Palace. One of the panellists, Ayesha Hazarika, an equal rights campaigner, told me, 'The royal family are the absolute top of the British class system; it is the most elitist system on the planet. A lot of people of colour will think "good: it's high time that this system was opened up a bit more."'[92]

The institution has modernised, though you'd be forgiven for not noticing. The Queen went with tradition to marry a fellow blue-blood in Philip (a Greek and Danish prince) but Prince Charles married outside royalty to aristocrats. William cast his net further with Kate Middleton who was from a middle-class, rural family. Prince Harry went further afield to marry an American divorcee. The last time that happened was in 1936 when Edward VIII had to abdicate his royal title in order to marry his American divorcee, Wallis Simpson. Meghan Markle though has been embraced by both the royal and political establishment which shows how things have moved on, if glacially.

Prince Harry is unlikely ever to be king so he is under less pressure to conform than his elder brother, though he did still require permission from The Queen to marry Markle. He is particularly close to William and Kate so he will have significant influence on the way the monarchy develops, as will his wife.

The 'Fab Four' as they have been dubbed by the UK tabloids, co-ordinate their work through their court at Kensington Palace. When Harry moved in years ago, a royal source told me the office had been set up with a corporate structure. The 'principals,' as they are known, are treated as joint CEOs. Courtiers are there merely to advise. William, Kate, Harry and Meghan call the shots, which was perhaps a reaction to the system the boys were brought up in when aides exercised more control, to the frustration of their mother Diana.

The four are also equal partners in The Royal Foundation which brings together their charitable and campaign work. 'Working as a family does have its challenges,' conceded Harry at a Foundation forum in February 2018. He and William have had a lifetime to get used to that of course but not so for Middleton and Markle.

The world media turned out in force for the forum because it was our first opportunity to hear how Markle might take her public role forward. She had only been engaged to Harry for a few months and all we knew was that she had given up her acting career and cut all ties with the campaigns and organisations she had been associated with such as UN Women and World Vision. Royal sources assured me she had every intention of continuing her work on those issues but wanted to do so with a clean slate from her new, more high-profile position.

Markle was asked on stage about women finding their voice and she responded, 'You'll often hear people say, "Well you're helping women find their voices," and I fundamentally disagree with that because women don't need to *find* their voice. They have a voice. They need to feel empowered to use it and people need to be encouraged to listen.'

It was a clear statement of intent from Markle that she wasn't going to stop having opinions just because she was joining the most famous family in the world. People would probably have questioned her strength of character if she had done anything else but she did raise a few eyebrows when she added, 'and I think right now in the climate that we're seeing, with so many campaigns, with 'Me Too,' 'Time's Up,' there's no better time than now to continue to shine a light on women feeling empowered, and people really helping to support them, men included.'

#MeToo and #TimesUp are regarded by some as political movements which is territory royals are expected to avoid and this speaks to the challenge Markle now faces. She's eloquent, passionate and charismatic and that's endeared her to many but could create jealousy within the ranks, as Diana learned. If she then crosses the line into what could be construed as political interference then republicans will use it against her, increasing pressure on the family.

How would it go down if Markle repeated her views on Donald Trump, for example? During the 2016 US election campaign, she told *The Nightly Show with Larry Wilmore*, 'Yes of course Trump is divisive,' and then went on to call him 'misogynistic.' She said she 'might just stay in Canada' if Trump won the presidential election, which of course he did.[93]

As a senior member of the royal family, Markle is expected to represent the monarch, potentially even hosting President Trump. That role is only tenable if she avoids party politics. Who knows who she will be asked to meet by government in future?

The Queen appoints the prime minister, she approves legislation and awards national honours. Any suggestion of political allegiance could threaten the crossbench support she relies on in Parliament which is the one body with the authority to unseat her. The Queen's impartiality is so essential she doesn't even exercise her right to vote, or show any sign that she would ever draw on her so-called 'reserve' powers.

If there is an election with no clear outcome and co-alition talks break down, she could, in theory, step in to call a fresh election but the last time we came close to that was in 2010 and the palace made it abundantly clear The Queen had no intention of getting involved and that she wasn't even in London. It was confirmation, if any were needed, that the monarch has no role or say in the formation of governments or the calling of elections and her family are expected to be mindful of that as her regular stand-ins.

The Queen is also Head of the Armed Forces, the Judiciary, Civil Service and is Supreme Governor of the Church of England. She can't be all things to all those pillars of the democratic system if she shows any fear or favour. She's floated above her multiple roles impeccably and the greatest demonstration of that for me was her state visit to the Republic of Ireland in 2011.

The UK and Ireland are close allies and neighbours but they also have a long history of violent territorial disputes and political infighting. She had to navigate through that on behalf of both nations, and it was personal for her too.

Ireland declared independence from Great Britain in 1922 and the island itself was split between Northern Ireland, which remained part of the UK, and the Republic. But tensions continued with Irish nationalists wanting the whole island reunited under Irish rule and union-ists wanting to keep things as they were. About 3,000 lives were lost over three decades in a conflict known as 'The Troubles.' The Queen's own beloved cousin, Lord Mountbatten – a decorated military officer – was killed by an Irish Republican Army bomb in County Sligo in 1979.

Successive British and Irish governments tried and failed to end the conflict until a political settlement was finally reached in 1998 with the 'Good Friday Agreement' which created a power-sharing assembly to govern Northern Ireland with cross-community consent.

A decade on from the accord, London and Dublin were ready to mark the normalisation of relations and needed a non-political figure of the right stature to symbolise the landmark moment. All eyes looked to The Queen and she boldly accepted. She would be the first British monarch to step foot in the Republic since her grandfather, George V, in 1911 when it was still under British rule. The mere announcement of her visit felt seismic.

One false word or gesture and she could re-open old wounds and undo years of painstaking diplomatic work. The stakes were incredibly high on all sides.

A series of engagements was organised on her behalf, taking into account the deep sensitivities on all sides.

She laid a wreath at Croke Park where, on 'Bloody Sunday' in 1920, British forces opened fire at a football match killing 14 people. The gesture was a public acknowledgement of past wrongs committed during Britain's rule. She didn't need to say anything, but there was healing in what she did and how she presented herself.

At a banquet that night in Dublin Castle, the former seat of British power, Elizabeth gave a speech and opened it in Irish. There were gasps in the room for the clear act of deference to an independent Irish state. She went on to offer her 'sincere thoughts and deep sympathy' to the victims from both sides in the conflict, which was as close to an apology as she was able to go and enough to earn her a standing ovation at the end from guests across the political divide.

In her reply, the Irish President, Mary McAleese, described The Queen's visit as 'a culmination of the success of the Peace Process.'[94]

The next year, Elizabeth followed up with a trip to Northern Ireland where she shook hands with the Deputy First Minister, Martin McGuinness, who was allegedly an IRA commander at the time of Mountbatten's death. You would never know how loaded that moment was for either of them when you take in the images.

The Queen is often held up as a model head of state but she also has a secondary role as Head of Nation which is where she's made herself almost indispensable.

According to her website, 'The Sovereign acts as a focus for national identity, unity and pride; gives a sense of stability and continuity; officially recognises success and excellence; and supports the ideal of voluntary service.'[95]

That explains the regular appearances at the State Opening of Parliament and Royal Ascot, for example. They make her part of the rhythm of public life. That's also why she steps in to represent the nation in times of celebration, such as the triumphant 2012 London Olympics, and of disaster.

The fire at Grenfell Tower in London in 2017 traumatised the country and only The Queen was able to articulate that when she visited survivors and first responders. The story had evolved by the time she arrived, after it emerged that those living on the estate had repeatedly complained about fire safety standards but to no avail. It very quickly turned in to a debate about rich and poor, the haves and the have-nots and most of those affected by the blaze were firmly at one end of that scale. The Queen was at the other which is why it was so extraordinary that she managed to connect with people on the ground that day. It helped that she was able to compensate for a previous visit by Prime Minister Theresa May who had been vilified for surrounding herself with security and only meeting those managing the response rather than victims.

'A Tale of Two Leaders' headlined the *Daily Mirror* alongside two contrasting images – one showing May surrounded by a ring of police and the caption, 'Protected.' The other showed The Queen listening to members of the community, captioned 'Concerned'.[96]

Elizabeth has an uncanny ability to judge when her presence will help rather than hinder. She doesn't need to say anything; she just needs to be there and show empathy. She has signposted her way through much of her public life in this way. Speeches and words play a relatively small part in her communications strategy.

A motto often attributed to Elizabeth is, 'I have to be seen to be believed,' and that explains why she wears those bright colours that mark her out in the crowd. When she meets a member of the public, she typically asks if they have come far and by the time they have answered an aide has ushered her on. She's created a memory for life for that person but, crucially, hasn't given away anything of herself. She's also created a powerful image for the media to use showing her amongst the people. This was the monarch who popularised the royal walkabout and it wasn't by accident.

The Queen created more opportunities to get out there and meet people when she formalised the support of voluntary service in to her job description. It allowed her and her family to link up with charities and causes they care about and show some character. Without that,

The Cambridges and Prince Harry wouldn't have been able to start the 'Heads Together' campaign to reduce the stigma of mental illness which has had a palpable effect on attitudes in the UK. The brothers used it as an opportunity to open-up about the trauma of losing their mother.

'Our grandparents, The Queen and The Duke of Edinburgh, had made support for charity central to their decades of service to the nation and the Commonwealth,' The Duke of Cambridge told the Royal Foundation forum. 'The task for us would not be to reinvent the wheel. Instead, our job was to follow the example of those who had come before us, to hold on to the values that have always guided our family, but also to seek to engage in public life in a way that was updated and relevant for our generation.' In other words, to continue the conversation his grandmother picked up on.

William gave a demonstration of that 'updated' monarchy when he left hospital with his wife and new born son and heir, Prince George, in July in 2013. He had his sleeves rolled up and carried the car seat himself, clicking it in to position before driving off with his new family. That doesn't sound extraordinary but just a generation ago, when Prince Charles did the same thing with William as a baby he wore a suit and tie and took the back seat of the car as a chauffeur drove them all off.

I interviewed William a couple of weeks after George's birth at Kensington Palace. He was still in that exhausted yet elated stage of early fatherhood. 'I blubbed for about half an hour when George was born,' he told one of the producers. 'It was ridiculous.'

I then asked him about his approach:

William: Where I can be, I am as independent as I want to be, same as Catherine and Harry. We've all grown up differently to other generations and I very much feel if I can do it myself, I want to do it myself. And there are times when you can't do it yourself and the system takes over or it's appropriate to do things differently. But, I think driving your son and your wife away from hospital was really important to me. And I don't like fuss, so it's much easier to just do it yourself.

Me: And you didn't stall.

William: I didn't stall; well it's an automatic so it's alright.

Me: The interpretation of the imagery we saw there, which went around the world, was that this was a modern monarchy and a new way of presenting the monarchy, but was it that? Are we reading too much into it? Is it just you doing it your way, you and your wife doing it your own way?

William: I think so; I'm just doing it the way I know, you know. If it's the right way, then brilliant, if it's not, if it's the wrong way, then I'll try to do it better, but, no... I'm reasonably headstrong about what I believe in and what I go for, and I've got fantastic people around me who give me great support and advice.

William admitted that he wasn't comfortable in front of the cameras. He accepts the public has a right to updates on the family but also that there's a line the media shouldn't be allowed to cross. The clearest sign of that came when he and his wife took court action against those responsible for taking and publishing topless pictures of

The Duchess on holiday in France in 2012. I met them when the pictures were published, during their official tour off the Solomon Islands in the South Pacific. She was upset, he was angry. It took nearly 5 years of legal proceedings, but the couple did eventually win damages and that sent a very clear message to the media not to try the same thing again.

'One lesson I've learned is, you never let them in too far, because it's very difficult to get them back out again,' William told a documentary team in 2017. 'You've got to maintain a barrier and a boundary.'[97] That was a lesson learned from his mother. 'I believe that she cried more about press intrusion than anything else in her life,' he told another film crew the same year.[98]

There are, no doubt, some very appealing trappings that come with being royal but there's also some sacrifice. Robert Hazell and Bob Harris at University College London wrote to that in a 2016 paper, 'The Queen, Prince Charles and Prince William have to abandon freedoms which the rest of us take for granted. Freedom of privacy and family life; freedom of expression; freedom to travel where we like; free choice of careers; freedom of religion; freedom to marry whom we like. For the royal family these basic human rights are all curtailed. The question is whether future heirs are willing to make the self-sacrifices required of living in a gilded cage.'

The authors argue that relentless invasions of privacy by the press are putting so much pressure on the family that they may come to question whether it's all worth it.

'Prince Charles and his sons have been the main victims, with Prince William and the Duchess of Cambridge now caught up in celebrity culture. The media are insatiable, and also fickle; if the popularity of the monarchy comes to depend on the support of the press, that Faustian pact may prove in the long run to be the greatest threat to the future of the monarchy.'[99]

Perhaps there is such a thing as too much clout? If anyone has tested the boundaries of that, it's The Queen. It was either that though, or risk losing her relevance and letting The Crown slip away which would leave her nothing to pass on. She would have failed in her duty.

Charles, William and eventually George will need to find their own blend of clout to suit their character and generation. Representation of the people, inevitably moves on. The UK's leading constitutional expert, Professor Vernon Bogdanor, argues, 'The monarchy cannot be exempt from change, and perhaps the central change has been a shift in attitude towards it from the mystical monarchy to the public service monarchy.'[100]

It was Elizabeth that engineered that shift and overhauled the entire royal brand as a result, disrupting an ancient and hallowed institution with few people noticing. In a speech to mark The Queen's Diamond Jubilee, then Prime Minister, David Cameron, told Parliament, 'She has moved the Monarchy forward. It has been said that "the art of progress is to preserve order amid change and change amid order", and in this the Queen is unparalleled. She has never shut the door on the future; instead, she has led the way through it.'[101]

She's done it so long that she's Britain's longest serving monarch. The Duke of Edinburgh is the longest serving royal consort and The Prince of Wales is now the longest serving heir apparent. In ordinary life, Charles would have retired years ago. His challenge has been to find his own purpose and he's managed that by professionalising his own role, embracing the 'public service monarchy' with thousands of engagements and fundraising efforts. He's pushed the envelope, literally, on the family's political neutrality too by writing a series of so called 'black spider' memos to government ministers with his thoughts on policy, so-called because of The Prince's unique scrawl. He's expressed views on everything from climate change to urban planning.

In 2008, he complained that architects were indulging in a 'free for all that will leave London and our other cities with a pockmarked skyline. Not just one carbuncle, ladies and gentlemen, on the face of a much-loved old friend, but a positive rash of them that will disfigure precious views and disinherit future generations of Londoners.'[102]

We know what *he's* thinking then when he sees at a skyscraper and it's made him a much more divisive figure than his mother. A royal source assures me he has every intention of following her example and steering clear of expressing opinion in public when he does accede to the throne. He's aware that, as Head of State, he will be expected to act on the advice of his ministers, not on his conscience. Until then though, he has some room for manoeuvre perhaps and he's arguably been proven right on some of the issues he pioneered as a young man such as environmentalism and inter-faith dialogue that have since gone mainstream.

Charles' character famously came into question when his affair with Camilla Parker-Bowles came to light, followed by an acrimonious divorce from Diana. He paid tribute to the 'brilliant' way his second wife took on the 'real, real challenge' of defining her public role in an interview I did with him in Scotland, 2015. It's still not clear if the public is ready to have Camilla as Queen, though she will automatically receive the title on his accession.

Clarence House issued a statement in 2005 saying she would use the title of 'Princess Consort'[103] instead but my understanding is nothing will be confirmed until the day Charles becomes king.

When I hear talk of The Crown passing straight to The Duke of Cambridge, I don't detect any appetite from either of them for that to happen. The Prince of Wales has spent a lifetime preparing to rule and The Duke is busy coming to terms with his own clout and juggling a young family. Neither of them speaks publicly on the matter of succession for obvious reasons but both will be aware of the towering example they are expected to live up to in Elizabeth II. She kept herself at the heart of the national conversation and that's the cachet that underscores her clout.

Elizabeth II's Cloutfile

Cause: Representation of the people.

Credibility: Lived up to her 21st birthday promise and remained above politics.

Character: True to her cause throughout her reign.

Conversation: The relevance of monarchy.

Connection: She reflected public sentiment, literally.

Cachet: Arguably, the world's most revered head of state.

CHAPTER 7

YOUR CLOUT

'Everything you can imagine is real.'
attributed to Pablo Picasso, 1881 – 1973.

EACH OF THE PEOPLE I have written about in this book have all the 6Cs of clout, but they've found their own blend to suit their characters and circumstances. They may not always have been conscious of what they were doing but we can still learn from it and, having spent time with people who have clout, I am convinced anyone can increase their own.

It starts with finding your drive...

CAUSE

When I started writing this book, I assumed people with clout are driven by hope – they know what they want and strive towards it. Now, I think it's as much about fear – the fear of losing that hope and slipping back to a place they don't want to go. For Stormzy, that place was represented by 'the ends' and for Emin it was Margate.

It's not entirely clear where it was for Steve Jobs but he suggests it manifested itself in a fear of failure and embarrassment.

Find your drive

To find your drive, look in to yourself and identify the situation you never want to find yourself in. Where is that dead end? It might be as specific as Margate or abstract as not being able to afford something that matters to you. I'm not a psychologist or a counsellor and I can't resolve your issues but we all have insecurities and the secret is to use them as a source of strength rather than letting them drag you down. The most successful people I know are some of the most insecure. They use that energy to drive themselves forward and make the sacrifices necessary to get to the top. You might not want to take it that far but, if you're still reading this book, I suspect you want more clout and that means you need to identify that drive. Then you need some direction and that's where the hope comes in…

What's the ambition?

What's your ultimate goal? Steve Jobs was seeking enlightenment. Emin aspired to be a seminal artist. The Queen was bidding to save the monarchy. You're not going to get to where you want to be straight away so you need to do it in steps. Do you need to become CEO? Or CFO? Are you better off breaking out on your own as an influencer? Do you simply want to be a social god?

Many of us think we are ambitious but we've lost direction along the way and our goals have become dated.

Circumstances change and so do we. You need to regroup and reset every so often and ask why you're doing it. Steve Jobs did that every morning in front of the mirror.

Don't hold back. Dream big. Jobs co-founded the most valuable company in the world from his garage, just as Steve Bezos did after him with Amazon.

Identify your target audience

You can't have clout if you don't have an audience and the people you need to listen are the ones who can help you achieve your goals. A wannabe CEO needs the backing of the board and shareholders, a politician needs an electorate and a blogger needs an active following.

Whose support do you need? It might be a small, specific group or an entire population. Once you know who they are, find out all you can about them. What are their hopes and fears? Which platforms are they on? What are they talking about there? Which names and brands are they associating with? It's less about their demographic profile and more about how they feel about life and what they want from it. You're looking for any indication of ambition so you can match yours with theirs.

What's the cause?

Once you know what you want and what your audience wants, you can identify the common ground and build your cause from there. The reality is, people don't support other people's ambitions - they have their own to worry about. You need to find something broad enough to appeal to everyone and takes them in their desired direction. Eva Kor preached forgiveness as a route to peace.

Steve Jobs championed the Information Revolution in his quest for enlightenment. Donald Trump wanted to 'Make America Great Again' so he and his audience could reclaim their pride.

CREDIBILITY

Your audience will only take you seriously if you appear credible so you need to assert your experience and expertise. Everyone in this book overcame seemingly insurmountable challenges in the name of their cause and that's what earned them respect.

Where's your experience?

You need a clear narrative. What are the hurdles you had to overcome to get where you are today? Where are you going to take it next? You need a story people can make sense of and follow.

Don't be held back by convention. We're all revolutionaries at heart and people will back you if they think you have a legitimate reason for wanting to disrupt the established order and if they have a stake in your success.

Where's your expertise?

It's worth noting that nobody in this book received a conventional education. They either dropped out of school, were kicked out or missed out altogether. That's all part of their story and adds to their credibility. Expertise is defined by the lessons you learned not how you learned them. Someone who suffered a miscarriage of justice can just as easily gain clout in the legal profession as a top law graduate. The self-trained Olympian is more inspirational that the one that was hot-housed from the age of two.

Own your platform

Once you have your story and you know which platform(s) you need to be on then you need to own it, with a view to lead. Stormzy threw himself into music and social media; Emin spent decades refining her art; and Kor travelled the world to become an accomplished speaker. They are all masters of their chosen platforms and that's underpinned by the passion they have for their cause. I think that's the secret to any great performance so forget about media and presentation training that purports to make you convincing. You need to feel convincing. You can apply that to meetings and office interactions or school pickups as much as the stage.

CHARACTER

Don't be afraid of showing that passion. If you don't care, why should your audience? Emotion is only a weakness if you lose control of it. Open-up and give them someone to identify with, then they will reciprocate and open-up to you. If you can also show some frailty, you'll make yourself even more human. Stop when it feels like you are unloading on your audience – nobody needs that. Don't bare your soul, just show the sides of your character that are relevant to your cause. It's about depth of character not breadth. It's also important to retain some mystique to make you interesting enough to come back to.

Be honest

If your audience picks up the slightest whiff of insincerity from you, they will instinctively pull back. You will give the impression of hiding something. They need to be in no doubt that you are being honest with them at all times. Even if they don't agree with you, they will respect you if they think your views are sincerely held.

Be consistent

You can undermine your character in a flash by contradicting your cause. The audience needs to be clear on what you stand for and what to expect from you. That applied to Emin as much as anyone else, even though she regularly shocked her audience. That's what they wanted from her. It was part of her narrative.

If you need to do a U-turn then be open about it and explain why it doesn't contradict your cause. That's where politicians so often go wrong. The worst thing you can do deny you went back on a promise when you clearly did. It shows bad character and nobody wants to be associated with that.

CONVERSATION

We talk, if not listen, to people all the time so we're already experts in conversation.

Commit to a conversation

Identify what your audience is talking about and narrow it down to the conversations that speak to your cause. Commit to the biggest one. The more universal the topic, the more of your audience you will reach. Emin spoke to intimacy, The Queen to representation.

CONNECTION

Now you are ready to connect.

Empathise with your audience

Donald Trump's base was angry and scared and he articulated that for them. If you can express how your audience feels then they will be able to identify with you and connect. Think of it as an exchange of sentiments where they realise they have something in common with you.

Offer a solution

Then help them resolve those sentiments. Trump promised to build a wall to make his audience feel safe again. The Queen showed Britons they can still be proud of their country despite the loss of the empire. Think of it as a collaboration. You're in it together and everyone has a stake in the result. What it shouldn't be, is a lecture. Nobody wants to be told what to think anymore. They will just drop you for someone who feels more engaging.

CACHET

Cachet is a status that other people desire. It delivers the charisma you need to attract and widen your audience and it comes from being the centre of conversation.

Own the conversation

To get there, you need to develop your other 5Cs to the point that nobody else can compete. You need the most compelling cause, the highest credibility, the strongest character, the best connection and most engaging conversation. As you attract attention and become more central to the debate you can start influencing its direction. If you take it towards your cause, you realise your clout.

To speed things along, imagine you already have clout. How are you carrying yourself? What are you saying and how are you saying it? If you can walk and talk like a leader, your audience will start seeing you as one. People love a rising star and will grab on to you if they think you will make it and will help them achieve their own ambition.

Health warning: Don't overplay your clout because you will appear arrogant; underplay it and you will come across as weak. If you listen to the audience you will find the right balance.

To retain your clout, keep going back to those 6Cs and identify any weaknesses that might be opening-up. Circumstances change; conversations move on, so keep regrouping and resetting to stay relevant. If in doubt, ask yourself how someone with clout would respond in that situation.

Keep ahead of your rivals by monitoring their 6Cs. No need to attack them on any weaknesses that open-up, just bolster your own clout in that area and you will gain the edge.

Now imagine a world where we all have clout. There are enough conversations to go around. We could all realise our potential. Whole organisations and communities would rise-up, the world would be a happier place and … well, that's another book, and depends on people using this one for the intended purpose, which is to make things better not worse.

For now, let's continue the conversation on my blog and see where it takes us. See you there.

https://www.cloutology.com/

ENDNOTES

1. Jobs, Steve. Macworld Conference & Expo. 9 January 2007.

2. DeCarlo, Scott. "The World's 25 Most Valuable Companies: Apple Is Now On Top." *Forbes*. 11 August 2011.

3. "Apple Unveils Higher Quality DRM-Free Music on the iTunes Store." Press Release. *Apple UK and Ireland*. 2 April 2007. London.

4. Jobs, Steve. "Thoughts on Music, Steve Jobs." Open Letter. 6 February 2007. http://www.apple.com/hotnews/thoughtsonmusic/ (deleted).

5. Jobs, Steve. Interview by David Sheff. "Playboy Interview: Steve Jobs." February 1985.

6. Jobs, Steve. Interview by David Sheff. "Playboy Interview: Steve Jobs." February 1985.

7. Jobs, Steve. "One Last Thing." *PBS*. 2 November 2011.

8. Jobs, Steve. Interview. "From 1993: What's Next? Steve Jobs's Vision, So on Target at Apple, Now Is Falling Short." *Wall Street Journal*. 25 May 1993.

9. Jobs, Steve. Interview by Jeff Goodell. "Steve Jobs: The *Rolling Stone* Interview." *Rolling Stone*. 16 June 1994.

10. Jobs, Steve. "Triumph of the Nerds." *John Gau Productions for Channel 4 and PBS*. 14 April 1996.

11. Jobs, Steve. Interview by David Sheff. "Playboy Interview: Steve Jobs." February 1985.

12. Jobs, Steve. "2005 Stanford Commencement Address." Stanford University. 12 June 2005.

13. Mazarakis, Anna & Shontell, Alyson. "Former Apple CEO John Sculley is working on a startup that he thinks could become bigger than Apple." 10 August 2017. *Business Insider.*

14. Jobs, Steve. "2005 Stanford Commencement Address." Stanford University. 12 June 2005.

15. Jobs, Steve. Interview by Steven Levy. "Good for the Soul." *Newsweek*. 16 October 2006.

16. Fiegerman, Seth. "Apple sells its billionth iPhone." *CNN*. 27 July 2016.

17. Hertzfeld, Andy. "Reality Distortion Field." *Folklore.* http://www.folklore.org/StoryView.py?story=Reality_Distortion_Field.txt.

18. Emin, Tracey. Interview by Sue Lawley. *Desert Island Discs*. BBC Radio 4. 3 December 2004.

19. Emin, Tracey. "Is Painting Dead." *Channel 4*, 3 December 1997.

20. "Taking a Turner for the worst." Commentary. *The Guardia*n. 4 December 1997.

21. Emin, Tracey. *Why I Never Became a Dancer*. 1995. Tate. Film.

22. Emin, Tracey. "Tracey Emin Interview." *Royal College of Art*. https://www.rca.ac.uk/studying-at-the-rca/the-rca-experience/student-voices/rca-luminaries/tracey-emin/.

23. Emin, Tracey. Interview with Melvyn Bragg. "Tracey Emin." *The South Bank Show*, ITV. 2005.

24. Emin, Tracey. "Tracey Emin Interview." *Royal College of Art*. https://www.rca.ac.uk/studying-

at-the-rca/the-rca-experience/student-voices/rca-luminaries/tracey-emin/.

25. Emin, Tracey. "Tracey Emin Interview." *Royal College of Art*. https://www.rca.ac.uk/studying-at-the-rca/the-rca-experience/student-voices/rca-luminaries/tracey-emin/.

26. Emin, Tracey. Interview by Will Self. "The Will Self interview: Tracey Emin, A slave to truth." *The Independent on Sunday*. 21 February 1999.

27. Joplin, Jay. Interview with Marcus Field. "The cubist: how Jay Jopling created the artist as superstar." *The Evening Standard*. 15 October 2009.

28. Emin, Tracey. Interview by Max Foster. "An un-made bed to make millions?" *CNN*. 27 June 2016.

29. Emin, Tracey. Interview by Sue Lawley. *Desert Island Discs*. BBC Radio 4. 3 December 2004.

30. Stormzy. "The eye of the Stormzy." *Channel 4 News*. YouTube. 1 August 2015. https://www.youtube.com/watch?v=idSMTACt6Lw.

31. Stormzy. Interview with Max Foster. *CNN International*. 22 & 23 February 2017.

32. Stormzy. Interview with Sam Wolfson. "Stormzy: 'My man Jeremy Corbyn! I dig what he says'" *The Guardian*. 21 May 2016.

33. Stormzy. "Shut Up." *YouTube*. https://www.youtube.com/watch?v=RqQGUJK7Na4.

34. Stormzy. Interview with Eleanor Halls. "Stormzy: The 22-Year Old MC Making Grime Cool Again." *GQ*. 16 August 2016.

35. McIntosh, Steven. "Stormzy at number one: Seven things you need to know about the grime artist." *BBC*. 2 March 2017.

36. Stormzy. Interview with Sam Wolfson. "Stormzy: 'My man Jeremy Corbyn! I dig what he says'" *The Guardian*. 21 May 2016.

37. Stormzy. Interview by Mark Savage. "BBC Sound Of 2015: Stormzy interview." *BBC News*. 7 January 2015.

38. Stormzy. Interview by Miranda Sawyer. "Stormzy: 'Respect me like you would Frank Ocean or Adele." *The Observer*. 19 February 2017.

39. Stormzy. Interview by Mark Savage. "BBC Sound Of 2015: Stormzy interview." *BBC News*. 7 January 2015.

40. Stormzy. Interview with Tom Lamont. "Stormzy: 'If it doesn't add up I give it to God." *GQ*. 15 July 2017.

41. Stormzy. Interview with Sam Wolfson. "Stormzy: 'My man Jeremy Corbyn! I dig what he says'" *The Guardian*. 21 May 2016.

42. Stormzy. Interview with Hattie Collins. *This is Grime*. Hodder & Stoughton. 2016.

43. Stormzy. Interview with Eleanor Halls. "Stormzy: The 22-Year Old MC Making Grime Cool Again." *GQ*. 16 August 2016.

44. Stormzy. Interview by Miranda Sawyer. "Stormzy: 'Respect me like you would Frank Ocean or Adele." *The Observer*. 19 February 2017.

45. Stormzy. Interview by Mark Savage. "BBC Sound Of 2015: Stormzy interview." *BBC*. 7 January 2015.

46. Wiley. Interview with Max Foster. *CNN International*. 22 & 23 February 2017.

47. Duggins, Alexi; Keens, Oliver; & Fraser, Tom. "A brief history of grime." *Time Out London*. 9 May 2016.

48. Ross, Daniel. "Stormzy's freestyle at the Brits proves he's a true virtuoso." *Classic FM*. 22 February 2018.

http://www.classicfm.com/music-news/stormzy-brits-2018-analysis/.

49.   "PM speech on housing to set out changes to planning rules." Press Release. *The Prime Minister's Office*. 4 March 2018. https://www.gov.uk/government/news/pm-speech-on-housing-to-set-out-changes-to-planning-rules.

50.   Stormy. Interview with Joseph JP Patterson. "Stormzy: Grime's Highly Favoured, Chosen One." *Complex*. 24 March 2015.

51.   Stormzy. Interview with Eleanor Halls. "Stormzy: The 22-Year Old MC Making Grime Cool Again." *GQ*. 16 August 2016.

52.   Kor, Eva. "At age 10, she was a human guinea pig." *CNN*. 22 January 2015.

53.   Kor, Eva. "CNN Inspirations: Incredible Survivors -- Eva Kor." *CNN*. 20 December 2016. https://edition.cnn.com/videos/world/2016/12/20/eva-kor-cnn-inspirations.cnn.

54.   Kor, Eva. "CNN Inspirations: Incredible Survivors -- Eva Kor." *CNN*. 20 December 2016. https://edition.cnn.com/videos/world/2016/12/20/eva-kor-cnn-inspirations.cnn.

55.   Trump, Donald (@realDonaldTrump). "The media and establishment want me out of the race so badly - I WILL NEVER DROP OUT OF THE RACE, WILL NEVER LET MY SUPPORTERS DOWN! #MAGA." 8 Oct 2016. 12.40 p.m. Tweet.

56.   Johnson, Jenna. "'I learned because of Fred': Trump cites brother's struggle in talking about addiction." *The Washington Post*. 26 October 2017.

57.   Trump, Donald. "Full text: Donald Trump announces a presidential bid." *The Washington Post*. 16 June 2015.

58.   Trump, Donald. Press Conference. Trump Turnberry. 31 July 2015.

59. Trump, Donald. Interview with Max Foster. "Donald Trump: Crimea is Europe's problem." *CNN*. 31 July 2015. YouTube. https://www.youtube.com/watch?v=haJeTeOuK4Q.

60. Trump, Donald. "Trump: 'I'll build the wall and Mexico's going to pay for it.'" *CNN*. 31 July 2015.

61. "Here's Donald Trump's Presidential Announcement Speech." *Time*. June 16, 2015.

62. Trump, Donald. Quoted by Alexander Mooney. CNN. "Trump says he has doubts about Obama's birth place." *CNN*. 17 March 2011. http://politicalticker.blogs.cnn.com/2011/03/17/trump-says-he-has-doubts-about-obama%E2%80%99s-birth-place/.

63. Trump, Donald. (@realDonaldTrump) "Sorry losers and haters, but my I.Q. is one of the highest -and you all know it! Please don't feel so stupid or insecure,it's not your fault." 6:37 PM - 8 May 2013, 6.37pm. Tweet. https://twitter.com/realdonaldtrump/status/332308211321425920

64. Trump, Donald. Quoted by Kurtis Lee. "Donald Trump's immigration stance divides, inflames and inspires." *Los Angeles Times*. 12 July 2015.

65. Trump, Donald. "Donald Trump's Argument For America." *Team Trump*. YouTube. 6 November 2016. https://www.youtube.com/watch?v=vST61W4bGm8.

66. Trump, Donald (@realDonaldTrump). "If the disgusting and corrupt media covered me honestly and didn't put false meaning into the words I say, I would be beating Hillary by 20%." 14 Aug 2016 5.37 a.m. Tweet.

67. Diamond, Jeremy. "Trump issues defiant apology for lewd remarks — then goes on the attack." *CNN*. 8 October 2016.

68. Diamond, Jeremy. "Trump issues defiant apology for lewd remarks — then goes on the attack." *CNN*. 8 October 2016.

69. Green, Joshua & Issenberg, Sasha. "Inside the Trump Bunker, With Days to Go." *Bloomberg*. 27 October 2016.

70. Luhby, Tami. "How Hillary Clinton lost." *CNN*. 10 November 2016. http://edition.cnn.com/2016/11/09/politics/clinton-votes-african-americans-latinos-women-white-voters/index.html.

71. Bump, Philip. "Donald Trump will be president thanks to 80,000 people in three states." *The Washington Post*. 1 December 2016.

72. Kushner, Jared. Interview with Steven Bertoni. "Exclusive Interview: How Jared Kushner Won Trump The White House." *Forbes*. 22 November 2016.

73. Trump, Donald. "Trump: I could 'shoot somebody and I wouldn't lose voters.'" Jeremy Diamond for *CNN*. 24 January 2016. https://edition.cnn.com/2016/01/23/politics/donald-trump-shoot-somebody-support/index.html.

74. Rich, Frank. "The Upper Crust; Her Majesty's Lonely Service." *New York Times*. 15 November 1992.

75. Diana, 7 Days. *Sandpaper Films* for BBC 1. 27 August 2017. 7.30pm.

76. Press Association (@PA). "Princess Diana's funeral - which took place 20 years ago today - remains the most-watched British live TV event of all time, by some margin." 6 Sep 2017, 2.14 a.m. Tweet.

77. "Best-selling single." *Guinness World Records*. http://www.guinnessworldrecords.com/world-records/59721-best-selling-single

78. "9/11 and death of Diana top Britain's most memorable events list." Press Release. *BBC Press Office*. 24 January 2007. http://www.bbc.co.uk/pressoffice/pressreleases/stories/2007/01_january/24/radio4.shtml.

79. Blair, Tony. "Blair Pays Tribute To Diana." BBC News. http://www.bbc.co.uk/news/special/politics97/diana/blairreact.html.

80. *The Express*, *Mirror* and *The Sun*. Front pages. 4 September 1997.

81. Diana, 7 Days. *Sandpaper Films* for BBC 1. 27 August 2017. 7.30pm.

82. Diana, 7 Days. *Sandpaper Films* for BBC 1. 27 August 2017. 7.30pm.

83. Dimbleby, Jonathan. *The Prince of Wales: A Biography*. Little Brown.

84. "A speech by the Queen on her 21st Birthday, 1947." *The Royal Family*. https://www.royal.uk/21st-birthday-speech-21-april-1947

85. Cameron, David. Parliamentary address for the Diamond Jubilee. 7 March 2012. The House of Commons. London.

86. "About Us." *The Commonwealth*. http://thecommonwealth.org/about-us

87. Turnbull, Malcolm (@TurnbullMalcolm). "Although I am a Republican, I am also an Elizabethan. It was an honour to meet Her Majesty today at Buckingham Palace." 11 Jul 2017, 7:46 a.m. Tweet.

88. Danish queen reflects on 40-year reign. *CNN*. http://edition.cnn.com/videos/world/2012/01/12/foster-denmark-queen-jubilee-reign.cnn.

89. Rosen, Andrew. *The Transformation of British Life 1950-2000: A Social History*. Manchester University Press. 2003. Chapter 3, p41.

90. Pool copy. Craithie Kirk. 14 September 2014. Aberdeenshire.

91. Helen Mirren. "LIVE from the New York Public Library." 27 April 2016.

92. CNN International. "Prince Harry is engaged to American actor Meghan Markle. CNN Talk is at Buckingham Palace: What do you think this means for the monarchy?" *Facebook*. https://www.facebook.com/cnninternational/videos/10155913981064641/.

93. Guardian News. "What Meghan Markle thinks of Donald Trump – from the archive." *YouTube*. https://www.youtube.com/watch?v=FgvV0R1n1W8.

94. "Full text of President Mary McAleese's speech." The Irish Times. 18 May 18 2011.

95. "The Role of Monarchy." *The Royal Family*, https://www.royal.uk/role-monarchy.

96. "A Tale of Two Leaders." *Daily Mirror*. 17 June 2017. Front page.

97. *Diana, Our Mother: Her Life and Legacy*. Oxford Film and Television for ITV. July 2017.

98. *Diana, 7 Days*. Sandpaper Films for BBC 1. 27 August 2017. 7.30pm.

99. Hazell, Robert and Morris, Bob. *The Queen at 90: The changing role of the monarchy, and future challenge.* University College London.. June 2016. p29-30.

100. Bogdanor, Vernon. "The Queen at 90." Gresham College. 18 April 2016. London.

101. Cameron, David. Parliamentary address for the Diamond Jubilee. 7 March 2012. The House of Commons. London.

102. HRH The Prince of Wales. "A speech by HRH The Prince of Wales at the New Buildings in Old Places Conference, St James's Palace, London." 31 January 2008 .

103. *The Wedding of His Royal Highness The Prince of Wales & Mrs Camilla Parker Bowles*. Media Pack. Clarence House. London. 2005.